"*Leaders Who Coach* brings a power to leadership, one that's supported ~~by both psycholog~~ logical research and business results. It provides superb coaching tools to engage the mentee's intrinsic motivation, which makes it a must-read for leaders who want to be successful with today's culturally and generationally diverse workforce."

—**Jorge Cherbosque, PhD,**
Lee Gardenswartz, PhD and Anita Rowe, PhD, authors of
Emotional Intelligence for Managing Results in a Diverse World

"*Leaders Who Coach* is a powerful guide for any leader who wants to make a profound difference in the lives of their employees and their organization as a whole. Jan Salisbury's accessible formula for adopting a coach approach to leadership is practical, inspiring, and empowering. I finally have a tool that I can share with the executives I coach that has the potential to revolutionize their impact."

—**Lisë Stewart**
Principal-in-Charge, Center for Individual and
Organizational Performance Eisner Advisory Group LLC

"*Leaders Who Coach* gives you freedom from having to know the answer to every question that shows up at your door (and the dread that accompanies that). It's a framework for coaching your team to be more capable, smarter, and more powerful after every visit to your office and every coaching conversation. Jan's craftsmanship and love of coaching brings an actionable system (used by every one of our leaders) that builds on strengths and capabilities, rather than what's wrong."

—**Pete Ness,** Founder, Pingman Tools

"Farming and ranching brims with leaders whose highest value is independence, and yet our livelihoods depend on a high degree of internal and external collaboration. This book powerfully presents how families in agriculture and leaders everywhere can learn to listen, coach each other, and lead from positions of vulnerability. I could have used it during the forty years of leadership in schools and agriculture."

—Carol Parker, MEd,
Founder Western Colorado Food and Farm Forum,
Valley Food Partnership, and the Parker Ranch.

"Here's your practical, potent, and inspiring guide to tapping into the ideas, thoughts, wisdom, and brilliance that is right in front of you—your team! Jan has expertly crafted an easy-to-follow guide that will support you in leveraging the enormous power of coaching. We've got more than enough 'tellers and knowers,' when what we need are leaders who coach."

—Alison Hendren, MCC
Founder and CEO, Coaching Out of the Box®

"A must-read for all leaders. Jan's expertise in both leadership and coaching come together in this book to offer specific examples that powerfully illustrate the coach approach in a way that's relatable and easily translated to practice. This book makes coaching accessible for anyone who wants to up their leadership game and support the growth of those they lead in meaningful and inspiring ways."

—Lerae Gidyk, Master Certified Coach,
Soul Designs Coaching Founder Canada

"If you want to be the kind of leader who empowers your people, team, and organization to thrive, read this book. Through this highly accessible and hands-on book, Jan will accompany you with encouragement, questions, and suggestions based on her thirty years' experience as a Master Coach to leaders. The journey to become a 'leader who coaches' may not be a thousand miles long, but it does begin with a single step. Take yours now."

—**Dr. Declan Woods**
Top team psychologist and CEO Coach,
CEO, teamGenie® and creator of teamSalient®
Global Head, Team Coaching, The Association for Coaching

"I've worked with Jan Salisbury for twenty-plus years in various stages of leadership. The Fire Service is militaristic on the fire ground—something that's required to keep everyone as safe as possible. But leading in the firehouse, the day-to-day personal interactions, requires a different approach. Learning how to effectively coach and not manage fire department employees has been an invaluable skill set. Over the past few years, I've introduced Jan to other fire department officers who have found similar success in their professional development. I highly recommend this book if you're interested in further developing your coaching skills."

—**Mark Niemeyer,** *Fire Chief, Boise Fire Department*
Vice-President, Western Fire Chiefs Association

"The coaching skills I learned from the program in this book completely changed the way I approached leading my team and will change the way you lead your team as well. It offers fantastic skills that will change all your relationships at work for the better. A must-read for leaders wanting to grow their teams and increase their impact."

—**Alyson Powell Erwin,**
Vice President of Product, Healthwise

"When you show up differently as a leader, you create an opportunity for every employee to flourish. Jan creates a pathway to develop yourself as a leader while providing examples of how leaders have found success as leaders who coach. She uses three primary skills of coaching to build into a coaching roadmap. The coaching roadmap is aligned with the International Coaching Federation (ICF) and provides visual guidance for the foundation of coaching. Read and dive into each chapter's NEXT section. It's an opportunity to dig deeper into your own coaching mindset."

—**Katie Schimmelpfennig**, RN, MS, Healthcare Leader

"If you're a leader, you're a coach—at least you should be. In *Leaders Who Coach*, Jan Salisbury offers helpful reminders for leaders who've already discovered the power of coaching. For leaders who are starting their coaching journey and are seeking to elevate the performance of those around them, Jan's book is a roadmap filled with plenty of practical coaching concepts and models."

—**Greg Bustin,** Vistage International Master Chair,
Author of *Accountability: The Key to Driving
a High-Performance Culture*

LEADERS
WHO COACH

LEADERS WHO COACH

THE ROADMAP TO UNLEASHING TEAM GENIUS

JAN SALISBURY

Stonebrook Publishing
Saint Louis, Missouri

A STONEBROOK PUBLISHING BOOK

©2022 Jan Salisbury

The Gottman Feeling Wheel in Appendix B is printed
with permission from the Gottman Institute.

Library of Congress Control Number: 2022906462

Paperback ISBN: 978-1-955711-12-8

eBook ISBN: 978-1-955711-13-5

www.stonebrookpublishing.net
PRINTED IN THE UNITED STATES OF AMERICA

DEDICATION

This book is dedicated to my husband, John Connors, who was always positive and never lost faith in my ability to write it, and to my daughter, Cameron Cook, whose encouragement and role model remind me to contribute to a better world every day.

CONTENTS

DEDICATION ix

PREFACE xiii

1.   WHY LEADERS MUST COACH—AND WHY NOW 1

2.   COACHING CHANGES THE COACH, TOO. 5

3.   CHANGE YOUR LEADERSHIP:
     PUT ON YOUR COACHING HAT! 13

4.   WHY LEADERS DON'T COACH. 21

5.   PRESENCE: SHOW UP AS A LEADER WHO COACHES 29

6.   WHEN YOU COACH, EVERYONE IS VULNERABLE. 37

7.   THREE COACHING SKILLS TO GET YOU THERE. 43

8.   THE ROADMAP FOR COACHING 63

9.   BEING COACHED: ONE STORY. 81

10.   COACH WHAT'S STRONG, NOT WHAT'S WRONG 87

11.   WHO OWNS ACCOUNTABILITY IN COACHING?. 99

12.   SEEK COACHABLE MOMENTS 107

13.   COACH TO IMPROVE PERFORMANCE 119

14.   THE COACH APPROACH TO UNLEASHING TEAM GENIUS . . 127

15.   COACHING THROUGH CHANGE, CRISIS,
      AND PANDEMICS 135

16.   COACHING DIFFERENCES. 147

17.   HOW COACHING CAN CREATE YOUR BEST CULTURE 153

18.   LEADER COACHING PRACTICES OF HIGH INTEGRITY:
      DO GOOD AND DO NO HARM. 167

19.   COACH ME TO COACH 175

APPENDIX A: KEY COACHING SKILLS 183

APPENDIX B: THE GOTTMAN FEELING WHEEL. 187

APPENDIX C: YOUR COACH ME PLAN. 189

ACKNOWLEDGMENTS. 193

NOTES 195

ABOUT THE AUTHOR 201

ABOUT LEADERS WHO COACH 203

PREFACE

ELEVEN YEARS AGO, I was coaching Derek, the president of a mid-size company. I was clear about affirming his strengths. "Everyone I spoke with told me your three top strengths were your vision of how the company could dominate a growing market, your belief in the positive impact of the company's mission, and the direct and powerful way you express yourself."

Derek smiled and then asked, "So what's the rest of it?"

"Well," I said, "sometimes those powerful strengths are overdone, and you can come across as someone who's so sure of yourself, you don't want to hear a different or challenging viewpoint. In other words, your delivery can shut down dialogue and innovation."

Derek reflected silently on the candid feedback I collected from his team, lamenting, "Wow, I had no idea."

I then asked Derek, "What kind of leader do you want to be? What do you hear in your team's input that's getting in your way?"

Derek looked down and then back up at me. "I want my team to feel like they can voice opinions, disagree, and creatively solve problems. I see now that my tendency to come across emotionally charged about mistakes and frustrations shuts them down. Yes, I can communicate directly, but I need to remove the perception that I'm upset or angry. Since I'm the president, my style clearly cascades down to the whole organization."

We then focused on what Derek was willing to change and where he could start. He recognized how important it was to follow through. Suddenly Derek stopped and said, "This coaching is very helpful—when my team and I coach others, we just tell them how we'd do it. You don't do that. Why can't I learn to coach like this?"

Why not indeed? I thought.

"That's an intriguing idea," I said. "I don't know why you and your team can't. Anyone can learn to coach, using the same behaviors and principles you're experiencing with me today." In that moment, the notion that leaders who coach could empower and develop others inspired me.

I've been an executive coach and consultant working with leaders and teams for over thirty years. Growing up as an army brat, much of my life was outside the United States, so it was natural for me to seek out and work with diverse companies and industries. I interacted with small, fledging entrepreneurs, as well as large, Fortune 500 companies and government entities. My industry work ranged from manufacturing to nonprofits, from agricultural to high tech, healthcare, utilities, and entertainment. I was equally at home with a world-renowned dance company or a fire department.

What I cared about most was working with leaders and teams who wanted to improve and learn to develop themselves and their organizations. I was, however, stuck in the consultant/expert model—I felt I had to know more than my clients to be of value to them. I was searching for a different way to support my clients' growth.

I decided to drop a lucrative part of my "expert" business and focus exclusively on developing leaders and teams. Coaching was still a new profession, and at the suggestion of a colleague, I plunged into an executive coaching program. I quickly realized that coaching was a mindset of partnering with my clients to help them discover what they wanted, what was possible, and how they could forge a path forward. It wasn't easy. I fumbled many times, feeling inept and ready to jump in with solutions before I learned to help my clients listen to themselves. I began to offer both consulting and coaching services, making sure my clients knew what they could expect from each approach. Both were valuable, but they weren't the same.

Coaching was an unchartered world for me as a professional, one filled with possibilities generated by my clients. I challenged myself to keep abreast of coaching research and knowledge, and eventually, I became a Master Certified Coach with the International Coaching Federation. To elevate coaching practices locally, I co-founded the first professional coaching association in Idaho. However, the real inspiration for connecting the skills and principles of professional coaching with coaching leaders came from the leaders I coached. Like Derek, they wondered if they could become leaders who coach. My goal was to listen to their needs and find a way to meet them.

My first challenge was to find a model of coaching that was both supported by professional coaching competencies and easy for leaders to learn. Then I met Alison Hendren, the CEO and founder of Coaching of the Box®. She had created the robust 5/5/5 model for coaching and had a proven track record with leaders.

Next, I sought a coach-facilitator partner who understood how to create an experiential learning environment, one with observation and feedback. Together with my co-founder, Dawn Monroe—former director of Leadership Development for Hewlett Packard's printing division—we created Leaders Who Coach. We asked ourselves, "How do we leverage what we know has worked well in other leadership development programs?"

We agreed on the following criteria:

- Create a safe environment where leaders could actively engage and learn experientially.
- Give them an opportunity to practice with real situations (not role-play).
- Allow them to experiment without fear of making mistakes.
- Encourage them to give and receive feedback from peers.

Our goal was to develop leaders who empowered their teams to solve problems and thrive. Most importantly, we wanted leaders to take what they learned and confidently apply it immediately. We wanted to create a program that intertwined coaching skills and leadership essentials. We called our first two-day intensive program *Leaders Who Coach: Essentials.*

Let me be clear: Derek and other leaders inspired my journey. They saw the value of executive coaching and grasped how coaching others could change their leadership and their organizations. I'm still learning from my clients. When leaders coach, they show up less as "leader as expert" and more as a "leader who empowers others to develop and contribute."

The leaders with whom I worked learned that to coach means adopting a mindset I call *the coach approach.* As this book will explore more fully, when you coach, you embody a deeper, more fundamental approach to the way you lead. The coach approach is present in every chapter of this book. The way you show up is to be present with someone. You focus on what's strong rather than what's wrong. You believe that people can grow and change and that mistakes are part of learning to be better. You realize you're not always the smartest person in the room and others provide knowledge, leadership, and solutions that, if respected, create great results. So, as you read this book, I encourage you not only to focus on skills but also reflect on your beliefs about others and leadership. These are the first steps to becoming a leader who coaches. If you're already a leader who coaches, may this book challenge you and encourage you to go deeper and empower others to soar and contribute.

Leadership and Coaching

What is a leader? Increasingly, we've discovered that people who lead do so in a variety of ways. They aren't always formal, designated leaders. They often lead by influence—influence acquired by stepping up to offer ideas, role-model values, or share their knowledge and expertise. They're the informal leaders of our workplaces, and they're the ones organizations should be mentoring and developing for their next leadership contribution. In the *Leaders Who Coach: Essentials* program, we believe that just as everyone is capable of coaching, everyone is also capable of leading.

Everyone who leads has an opportunity to develop and empower others every single day. Sometimes it's as simple as asking someone for their ideas and then listening to what they have to say. Sometimes it's facilitating a team to innovate a shared vision of the future. Leaders mentor to teach, delegate to develop, promote to stretch, and give constructive feedback to improve others. Great leaders know that cultivating people and teams is the key to sustained results. Why not equip leaders with the know-how and best practices endorsed in the coaching profession?

While we knew that the idea of teaching coaching to leaders was sound, Dawn and I were both surprised and excited about what happened in our first programs. When leaders were required to bring real workplace situations to our program, they experienced and saw the impact of coaching on themselves and others. When they gave and received feedback, they felt open to improving. When they listened deeply to others and challenged them to think and feel their way to solutions and insights, they felt triumphant. Most of all, they learned to shed their problem-solving personas and tap into the know-how of others. These leaders realized that coaching could ignite the often-untapped insights and experiences of others to achieve real results. They shared the joy when the person they were coaching lit up with awareness and found their way to resolution or the next step. Leaders who coach realized that as their team's capabilities expanded, they could capture the time and space to reflect and grow the business.

Leaders coach not only their direct reports but also their peers, teams, customers, and even their leaders. Derek, the company president who kick-started my idea, created a coaching culture when all his leaders became leaders who coach. Other leaders are following suit.

The genesis for this book emerged from leaders in our program who wanted more. They wanted to coach their teams more effectively and apply the skills and insights they learned throughout their leadership. However, there was a gap—a plethora of books on professional coaching, but slim pickings for leaders who coached. I knew the next step was to write a book that would support leaders and inspire them to coach.

This book is dedicated to the leaders who took a risk to change their leadership style and learn to coach. You wrote this book with me. Your experiences and insights spurred me forward. May this book remind you of what you do well and encourage you to grow to the next level.

To help you turn insight and understanding into action, each chapter will end with **NEXT**: questions, encouragement, and suggestions for you to try. NEXT is a step to propel you forward to become a leader who coaches. You choose that step and see how it works for you. Simply reading this book won't make you a leader who coaches but putting these ideas into practice will help you get there.

If you want to be a leader who coaches, may this book reward your curiosity and give you a place to begin your coaching practice. May it accompany you on your coaching journey, taking one idea or skill at a time that speaks to you.

WHY LEADERS MUST COACH—AND WHY NOW

"There is more intelligence inside our organizations than we are using."

—Liz Wiseman

WHAT'S DIFFERENT ABOUT the coaching approach we focus on in this book? It starts with the definition of coaching. I define *coaching* as focused, structured conversations that help develop others by stimulating greater awareness, deeper and broader thinking, and wiser decisions and actions.[1]

Early in our programs, we discovered that our participants defined coaching differently. Many leaders walked in (and still do) with a negative view of coaching. When we launched our program, professional coaching was still new, and *to be coached* had morphed into a catchphrase for telling someone they were underperforming and needed to improve—and quickly. For some, the word *coached* had the potential to shame, communicating, "You need to be coached." For some, being coached might be the beginning of being asked to leave their position.

Coaching seemed like a nicer way to deliver negative feedback. Only it wasn't nicer, just confusing. Alternatively, leaders saw coaching as telling someone how to solve a problem or what to do next. Unless they'd recently received the benefits of executive coaching, many leaders attending our program arrived with one of these definitions of coaching in the workplace. If your understanding of coaching falls somewhere within these definitions, this chapter will help you see that coaching is a distinct way to develop and lead others.

First, a little background. While the profession of coaching to help people grow and reach their goals is relatively new, the idea of coaching is not. Before the twenty-first century, *to coach* meant to transport people from where they were to where they wanted to be. Coaching was then linked to sports and experts who could help you learn something new. Anyone who has played organized sports or been coached by an experienced practitioner of a sport knows the value of a coach. They show, tell, and create experiences, so we can learn and perform. Finally, the human potential movement, which began during the 1960s, contributed to coaching by emphasizing that all of us have strengths that, if leveraged, could help us grow and perform.

In the early days of leadership coaching, consultants coached executives to fix or improve their leadership. Leadership consultants were often confidential advisors with whom the leader could bounce ideas and share challenges. Consultants also facilitated training, team building, strategic planning, and other interventions to increase effectiveness and skill development. In effect, consultants were adjunct experts and advisors. I know because I was one of them. This kind of expert help provides important support for leaders and organizations. But it isn't coaching.

Similarly, leaders have traditionally been promoted to the next level of leadership because they're experts and can "get 'er done." As organizations have flattened their organizational structure, they've realized that the best leaders entrust their teams to find the best strategies and solutions. The best leaders are humble and ask more than they tell.[2] These changes in the workplace have motivated leaders to seek out coaching as a fundamental leadership capability.

Leaders who coach lead by enabling others to use their inherent capabilities and experiences to make better decisions. As the title of this book exclaims, coaching unleashes the genius of your team. Each person has untapped abilities and gifts that are often hidden to them and to their leaders. The examples in this book are informed by the stories of hundreds of leaders who've adopted coaching as a way to cultivate their teams and culture. They are mosaics of stories told to me by leaders.

The skills, principles, and coaching process described in this book are also supported by decades of practice and research in the social sciences and professional coaching associations. When organizations adopt coaching as part of their culture, benefits accumulate. Results from a recent study of Canadian healthcare leaders and professionals who were trained in an evidenced-based coaching program yielded strong qualitative and quantitative results.[3] Pre- and post-surveys after training were analyzed and showed that participants:

- were more committed to sharing power with others
- developed employees for sustained improvement instead of waiting to address poor performance
- improved their listening and communication skills
- collaborated more with peers to deliver better solutions
- encouraged others to define action steps and accountability
- noticed that everyone increased their ownership of results
- realized an increase in innovation in problem-solving

There is no better time for leaders to adopt coaching as a vital leadership skill. Challenged to adapt to the ever-changing social, business and economic landscape, organizations understand that cultivating their team is essential for success.

NEXT

- How much time do you spend developing others? Is it enough?
- What are the primary ways you do so?
- How often do you ask for the ideas of others before you share your own ideas?
- How could you be more comfortable with not having the best idea or being the smartest person in the room?
- What would others say is a strength of yours as a leader?

COACHING CHANGES
THE COACH, TOO

*"We cannot change what we are not aware of,
and once we are aware, we cannot help but change."*

—Sheryl Sandberg

YOU MOST LIKELY picked up this book to discover how coaching could improve your leadership. Throughout this book, I offer research, examples, and case studies about the impact coaching has had on organizations and teams. To bring change to others, however, you must first change. Leaders who coach effectively shift the way they see themselves and the world. They learn that the first step in adopting a coach approach is to always be open to growing themselves.

Learn by Seeing through Multiple Perspectives

Your vision of what's possible changes when you coach—both directly and indirectly. If you're a leader who coaches, each coaching conversation expands your understanding. When you reach inside yourself to relate and empathize with views that are different and sometimes foreign to you, you grow. You're challenged to open up to new possibilities, motivations, and aspirations voiced by others. In the process, you gain a window into others' filters and interpretations of your organization that, try as you might, you can't easily access because your power as a leader insulates you. Finally, coaching naturally fosters collaboration and strengthens your partnership with others.

> When Jason became the new VP of sales, his CEO warned him that there were issues on the team and that he'd have challenges. "I want to be honest with you," the CEO said. "The reason I hired you was because the team isn't really a team, and they don't support one another. They work in silos. I want you to help them understand that they sink or swim together. The more they support one another and share their knowledge, the better results they'll enjoy. Their previous boss didn't understand that. He tried to motivate them strictly through his stories of success and his relationship with them."
>
> Jason knew he couldn't merely tell the team to change their behavior because they most likely would feel blamed. He reasoned that they knew more about the customer and the product than he did. He had to find a way to help them discover their strengths, both individually and as a team. He also knew this wouldn't be easy for a sales team that was used to competing against one another for sales numbers.
>
> Jason enrolled in our coaching program. As he practiced coaching, he noticed that when he focused on what others wanted or needed, he became more patient. When he listened to another person's perspective and goals, instead of trying to fix something or rushing to make it different, the other person became more engaged in defining what they might do to change things for the better.
>
> Later, he took a deep breath and shared with his CEO, "I think this team is very capable of teaching me about the business and creating a

shared way to do business. I'm going to begin by asking questions about what they want, what's working, and what's not. Then I'm going to invite them to paint a picture of a culture that will be the best for them and the company. Now that we're negotiating how to do business with COVID-19 still here, that's the approach I'll be taking."

While Jason wasn't entirely comfortable with not jumping in and telling his team what to do, he realized that this would foster distrust, not the sense of shared fate he and the CEO were seeking.

Learn about Yourself through Other People's Journeys

As you coach others, you also learn new things about yourself. Even as you listen to others, you reflect on your own experiences and challenges. While we differ in many ways, the human experience can transcend our differences when we listen to others.

I became aware of this when I was coaching another leader to procrastinate less. I immediately recognized her patterns of procrastination in myself. Didn't I do the same thing? Wasn't I attracted to the shiny balls of new things and innovative projects? Underneath my procrastination, wasn't there anxiety about how much time I wasted on something that wasn't interesting to me? As my client began to identify the beliefs that held her back and the strategies for moving forward, I couldn't help but reflect on my obstacles and options. When our coaching conversation ended, I asked myself, "What could I do differently?" I then shared with her what I'd learned from her.

When we coach, we hear the ways others find themselves stuck or challenged. When we work with others to change and improve, it's harder to judge them.

Lara was struggling with the feedback from her boss, Jerry. "You're a great problem solver, Lara. However, what I hear is that your team feels shut down because you dominate team meetings with your solutions. Look, there's a reason you hired a great team. Your job as a leader is to leverage their experience and knowledge."

Lara was shocked. "I've always been a great problem solver. I just thought that was my role as a leader. It sounds like you want me to work through my team more and stop leading from the front all the time."

"Exactly, Lara," Jerry responded. "Elicit and build on their ideas; don't tell them. Use the way we work together as an example."

Lara thought for a moment. "You're right. You don't tell me what to do. You help me get unstuck, clarify my goals, and then let me have at it. That's what I love about reporting to you."

How Research Supports Coaching

There's also a neurological component to coaching that transmits positive intent. Our brains are uniquely wired to relate and bond to one another. For example, some parts of our brain are uniquely tied to recognizing faces; then, through our cultures, we learn to ascribe meaning and emotions to those faces. I once heard an Italian scientist describe how scientists discovered mirror neurons in primates' brains.[4] Similar neurons with the same objective fired in one monkey when it observed another monkey doing something! Imagine—just seeing and hearing can stimulate our brains to feel the experience of another person. Many social scientists believe that mirror neurons and neuroplasticity were the keys to survival among stronger animals during our evolution. They enabled us to adapt and connect emotionally, using our collective strength as tribes to overcome powerful animals around us, according to Lisa Feldman Barrett.[5] So, when you coach, you're strengthening connections between you and your team. You're reinforcing the very bonds and collaboration that are at the heart of being human.

The journey to understanding how coaching correlates with brain functioning is just beginning. Recently, in a controlled experiment, students were exposed to two different coaching styles: one focused on assessing their performance and the other on what their ideal outcomes and aspirations would look like.[6] A functional Magnetic Resonance Imaging (MRI) machine measured their brain activity in a third interview in which students were asked how they felt after the two different coaching styles. Those who experienced the interviewer coaching style that focused on ideal outcomes reported more feelings of hope and inspiration than those focused on performance assessment. Areas of their brain that were stimulated included those related to empathy and emotional safety; big-picture, positive thinking; and visual processing. The researchers concluded that positive coaching that focuses on possibilities effectively activates the stress-reduction systems in the body. Specifically, stress reduction is facilitated because coaching encourages others to envision a desired future for themselves. Forward-thinking and defining positive outcomes are part of what distinguishes coaching from other forms of helping. As you'll learn, the coaching roadmap helps to positively motivate others to reach for a different outcome or future.

As a leader who coaches, you're engaging in an evidenced-based process that's positive, vision-based, and stimulates others to be open to possibilities and make lasting changes. Coaching illuminates what's important and meaningful to others, motivating them to tackle challenges and change.

The Coach Approach

Leaders often report that coaching is not only a valuable skill set but becomes a signature part of their leadership style. They develop a coach approach to leading. The coach approach begins with confident humility, having faith in one's capability while appreciating that one may not have the right solution or even be addressing the right problem.[7] As a result, leaders actively believe that their team members often have untapped knowledge and skills to reach their goals and address their challenges. Leaders become more curious and less the seat of knowledge or the source of what's best. More importantly, the people around them also become more confident. They seek out leaders, knowing they'll be listened to objectively and given an opportunity to stretch and solve their own issues. Leaders who embody the coach approach are curious about others' ideas and perspectives, and they listen carefully before they make decisions.

Reading this, you may be concerned that if you become a leader who coaches, your office will fill up with people seeking help. What actually happens is that others seek you out because they want to develop their skills and resolve dilemmas and challenges. They're more confident in themselves and in their relationship with you. Leaders also report that coaching takes less time in the long run. The visits to your office to ask you to fix things will decrease as others leverage their learning.

Coaching others can result in a shift in your focus as a leader. When you can spend less time in the shallows, you're able to reflect on where your ship is headed and can decide whether you have the right crew in the best roles. Thus, you're able to spend more time on the business, focusing on other crucial leadership tasks.

It can be very stressful to feel that you're responsible for all the knowledge and expertise needed to lead your company or team. Leading people doesn't mean you do everything. As Adam Grant suggests in his book, *Think Again*,[8] leaders who exhibit "confident humility" are more agile because they've discovered the joy of being wrong—they're more capable of learning and leading. I'm often asked, "How do I create a culture where others feel ownership for the business?" When you coach, people naturally accept that their issues are theirs and that their solutions are for them to discover.

What You Lose When You Coach

Finally, while becoming a leader who coaches has many benefits, change can also mean loss. What are you losing?

- You quit being the supreme problem solver.
- You set aside your ego so others can grow.
- You let go of perfectionism and the belief that you can do it better and faster.
- You let go of being the person who must know everything.

At the same time, you receive joy from watching others accomplish their goals. "At the end of the day, my leadership effectiveness is measured not by what I'm able to accomplish, but by what those whom I lead are able to accomplish."[9]

Becoming a leader who coaches will change you. It will transform your leadership and sharpen your vista of the world. As you develop and elevate others, the benefits to you and your organization spread. As you adapt the coach approach to leadership, you'll discover a new way to lead. As you dive into the skills and roadmap of coaching, you'll know how to help others grow every day.

NEXT

- How challenging is it for you to let go of being the chief problem solver? How would you feel if you let go of this? How would others feel?
- Identify some moments when you could hold back from giving a solution or expressing an opinion. Invite others to make suggestions and share their perspective.
- So far, what about being a leader who coaches appeals to you?

3

CHANGE YOUR LEADERSHIP: PUT ON YOUR COACHING HAT!

"A single approach to leadership, whether traditional or emerging, is not going to meet the myriad of challenges and pace of change today's leaders face."

—J. Jordon, M. Wade & T. Yokoi

LEADERS WHO COACH report that they've learned to intentionally put on their coaching hat. Think of all the hats you wear as a leader: strategist, visionary, accountability partner, mentor, decision-maker, negotiator—the list goes on. You often unconsciously switch hats as you adapt to the needs of the situation and your team. Each hat brings a different focus and communication style.

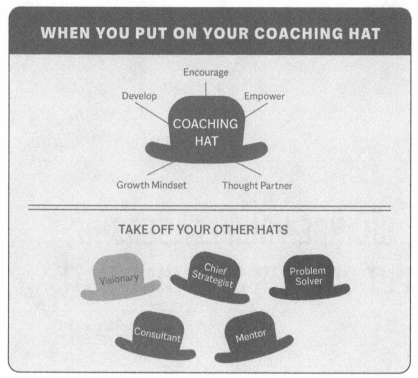

© 2021 Jan Salisbury

Leaders intuitively discover what studies have long supported: There's no single best leadership style because being an effective leader depends on the situation—on the goals, tasks, and relationships involved. As you assess the needs of your team members at that moment, you bring a different focus and skill set.

When you put on your coaching hat, you also show up differently as a leader. For many leaders, the coaching hat brings a new perspective to their leadership, and everyone around them feels the change.

This chapter describes some fundamental shifts leaders make when they decide to coach. What does it take internally to wear a coaching hat, and how might it change your leadership? Before we get to the nuts and bolts of coaching skills, let's focus on the values and beliefs that successful leaders who coach display.

The Growth Mindset

First, leaders who coach shift to a growth mindset. Your mindset is the way you approach life. Do you believe that we're all born with a hand of cards, and pretty much all we can do is play them out, depending on the cards others hold? Do you believe that talent is fixed and our ability to learn from mistakes is limited?

According to Carol Dweck, a research educational psychologist, a fixed mindset leads to giving up easily, covering mistakes, and being invested in being the expert.[10] When we have a fixed mindset, we can feel threatened by others' success and diminish the importance of feedback and effort. We believe we're who we are now, and not much is likely to change. According to Dweck's research, when the leaders of an organization view the world through a fixed mindset, they're less likely to coach their employees and more likely to create a culture where resources are hoarded by the talented. They also tend to hire those who aren't as skilled to preserve their exceptionalism.

On the other hand, when we lead with a growth mindset, we seek ways to improve; we seek challenges and feedback so we can learn from criticism. Growth mindset cultures foster trust, hard work, and positivity. These beliefs create a culture of possibilities. You might say that when you coach, you're always coaching what's possible. What goals are possible, what solutions are possible, and what future is possible. When you coach, you start by communicating to your team that you believe in their capabilities. Then you coach them to discover their path forward.

Marla was a new executive director of a nonprofit foundation. She'd come from a similar organization and knew how to accomplish results. But no matter whom she hired, she felt that they weren't up to the same standard of excellence she believed in. Her outside stakeholders were very happy with her, but her projects weren't getting completed because she couldn't do it all.

Her transition to being a leader who coached was rocky. She acknowledged that, deep inside, she employed a telling style. "They aren't following through, and I'm disappointed they can't complete things more quickly," she exclaimed to her coach.

She also doubted whether Steve, her director of marketing, could perform. In one meeting with an outside vendor, she found herself once again stepping in to define what should happen next. Then she stopped herself and stepped back. Turning to Steve, she calmly said, "I think the two of you know where you're going, and I look forward to hearing what you come up with." She held her breath. Steve looked surprised and nodded.

The next morning, Steve knocked on her door and presented new ideas for the project. It was the first time Steve had initiated a new plan. Marla realized that she hadn't really believed Steve could change. By stepping back and withholding her opinions, Steve heard Marla's confidence in him, and he stepped up. Marla described it as an aha experience in her journey to become a leader who coaches.

Most of us have learned to see the world through both fixed and growth mindsets. When you put the coaching hat on, you challenge yourself to reach toward a growth mindset. You remind yourself that believing in what's possible and in the ability of people to grow can inspire others to exceptional performance.

Empower and Develop

Finally, leaders believe that a fundamental *why* for their leadership is to grow others. Every day they look for opportunities to do so. They make time to meet with their team individually and in groups precisely to help them share their ideas, use their resources, and focus on the goals they've set for themselves and the organization. While leaders are ultimately responsible for reaching their results, they're invested in hiring and developing people who are committed to making the business successful, regardless of their position in the organization.

As the story goes, the president of IBM was visiting various sites. He was about to enter a secure computer research and development center with the department manager when the security guard stopped to ask him for his IBM badge. The department manager was mortified. "Don't you know who this is?" he asked.

"Well," said the security guard, "it's my job to make sure everyone has the proper access to enter, sir."

The IBM president looked at the guard and smiled. "That's exactly what I'd have done; here's my ID."

I love this example because, small as it is, it's a great example of the dynamic of ownership. The security guard clearly understood the importance of her role and owned it, even in the face of possible criticism. The president not only respectfully complied but also wholly and cheerfully supported her actions. It's reasonable to imagine that she left work that day feeling valued and more confident to do the right thing. That's also what happens when you coach. As a leader who coaches, you step out of being the authority and actively invest in entrusting others.

Shed the Expert Role

Effective leaders understand that what got you here won't get you there.[11] You may have been promoted for your business or technical acumen, but as you move up in leadership, you may quickly discover that your responsibility is less about being the expert problem solver and more about supporting, challenging, and promoting others to achieve results. You're not disengaged; you're engaged in a new way. You no longer see yourself as the hub of the team; you realize that your role is to create more connected spokes to strengthen the wheel of the team that moves everyone forward.

One leadership hat that's different from coaching but is instrumental in developing others is the role of mentor. Most of us have had mentors whose influence on our lives and careers has been significant. I single out the role of mentor because many in the workplace view the mentoring relationship as coaching. Mentors often coach, but we choose them as mentors precisely because they have relevant organizational experience and expertise, and we trust them to guide us in our career journey.

I had a wise teaching mentor in graduate school. John believed in my teaching ability and encouraged me to apply for a teaching assistantship. I was humbled by his suggestion and surprised that I enjoyed it. He modeled an inclusive teaching style, which I later emulated. He also shared his best teaching practices, such as creating tests that enhanced more than measured learning.

Next, John pointed out an opportunity for me to apply for a tenured position in psychology. I wasn't sure, but he believed in me when my belief in myself faltered. When I landed that college teaching position, I panicked. How could I teach topics about which I had so little depth of knowledge? In response, John shared stories about how he, too, had a steep learning curve when he began teaching. Gradually, I found myself sharing my joy and experiences with him. Teaching became a foundation in my evolving professional career.

I chose John as a mentor because I admired his teaching style and his unique approach to psychology. He challenged my assumptions about myself, but he also shared his own challenges. John also had mastered two important coaching skills: listening deeply and asking provocative questions to prod me into thinking deeply. His impact on me was profound.

However, John was my mentor, not my coach. As you'll discover in this book, when you coach, your focus is on helping the person being coached rely on their experiences, ideas, and resources so they can grow and reach their goals. While mentoring isn't coaching, your coaching skills can strengthen your impact as a mentor.

Putting On the Coaching Hat

How will it feel to put on a coaching hat? If you're like many of the leaders with whom I've worked, changing how you lead and learning a new approach or skill can feel challenging and uncomfortable. When leaders first learn to coach, there's often, directly or indirectly, an internal dialogue that resists change. *Why should I change? I won't be good at this. I'll feel incompetent and awkward. No matter what the research says, what if it doesn't work? It's easier to continue to be the leader I am. I'm good enough.* If you're reading this book, however, you're clearly interested in adding the coaching hat to your leadership and life. As you learn to coach, don the coaching hat as often as you can—one skill, one practice, one opportunity at a time.

Becoming a leader who coaches can benefit everyone around you—yourself, your team, and your organization. I'll share those benefits through stories recounted to me and a decade of research about leaders coaching. Your journey may be different. As you coach, you'll decide for yourself what it means to put on your leadership hat.

NEXT

- As you lead throughout your day, keep track of all the different hats you wear as a leader. Note when you put them on and why.
- What hats are most comfortable for you? With which hats do you feel you're in your element or strength?
- Identify moments when your coaching hat may be appropriate. When would helping others find their path to a solution without your advice serve both them and you well?
- What are the potential benefits to your organization if you and other leaders coach?

4

WHY LEADERS DON'T COACH

"Managers believe that they coach far more often than their employees believe they do."

—John Zinger & Kathleen Stinett

FOR MOST LEADERS, the coach approach to leadership changes the way we think and the way we behave, at least some of the time. That was even true for me as a professional coach as I made the transition from consulting and facilitating to coaching. Suddenly, I was unsure if I could offer value through coaching because I was so used to bringing expertise. It was easier to continue my old pattern since most clients were perfectly happy with my performance. However, I knew coaching could develop others beyond my expertise, and that goal was exciting.

Change often brings resistance—reasons why we can't change or anticipation that change will be too challenging or not positive. To be successful in changing a habit, change models encourage us to lean into the resistance. That means treating resistance as natural and healthy and finding ways to address whatever feelings and beliefs are impeding us.

When leaders learn to coach, I hear five common challenges to their ability to embrace coaching. I share the following stories to increase your awareness and inoculate the tendency to shift back to other leadership styles when coaching will work best for achieving your mission.

"I'm the Chief Problem Solver"

Joe's a new manager who's recently been promoted to assistant vice president of operations. He's known for his hard work, quick learning, and winning smile. When his CEO offered him a spot in our *Leaders Who Coach: Essentials* program, he was all in. After our first coaching demonstration, he blurted out, "I can't do that. I love solving problems, and I can't see how I can lead without doing it."

Think about your path to leadership. Were you a star expert in your field, increasingly rewarded with the next leadership position? You got the job done; however, being the lead problem solver can backfire. First, other team members aren't stretched to develop. Second, when you're the team leader *and* the chief problem solver, it creates a dynamic of everyone looking to you for direction and answers. The team's spirit is dampened. Their confidence to be bold, speak up, make mistakes, and tackle tough projects is undermined. Finally, a team that relies on the leader to solve all the problems isn't a team that's effective and interdependent. Recent studies have confirmed what you may already know: the best teams communicate with and leverage everyone on the team.[12] Cohesiveness and productivity rise.

To be honest, problem solving is fulfilling for us all. We've contributed something of value, and others see it and appreciate us. Our egos are stroked. That's hard to give up. How can we let go of the immediate rush of helping another person when we solve their problem? If we aren't solving problems, what purpose, we ask ourselves, do we have as leaders?

The crux of coaching is growing others and providing a culture that cultivates their best work and life. Imagine someone walking out of your office beaming because *they've* chosen the best way to improve or approach a challenging problem. How would that feel to you—and to them?

When Joe completed our Essentials program, he immediately dove in at the next team meeting, despite his fears about giving up his role as chief problem solver. Although his team was surprised that he didn't tell them what to do, they spoke up and shared their ideas about how to address a major issue. Joe was surprised that they communicated with one another more than usual at the meeting and were resolved to follow through by identifying who was accountable for what before they left the meeting. Joe was energized and emboldened. It was less work, he shared, and the solutions were creative and sustainable.

"I Don't Have the Time"

Leaders often imagine that coaching will suck up their time as they painstakingly guide others. It's so much easier, they think, to tell them the correct answer. I often present a brief role-play that we call *drive-by coaching*. It takes about five minutes and takes place in a hallway. Participants observe and write down what works and what doesn't. What works, they tell us, is that the leader doesn't tell the person what needs to be done. Instead, the leader helps the person explore what's most important to them and what they can do to improve or resolve the situation. Most importantly, participants repeatedly recognize that the leader in the role-play doesn't own the problem. As a result, there's no monkey on their back. And the conversation only takes five minutes.

How much time is it worth to enable someone else to create a plan, become aware, or get unstuck? It's an investment that keeps on paying.

Once your team knows they have the capability to contribute and find solutions as individuals and as a team, it's a gift that keeps on giving—to them, you, and your organization. Your team members come to interactions prepared to engage and partner with you, their leader.

> *McKinsie manages six software developers, and they've come to trust her judgment and ability when they find themselves knee-deep in software hell. She's a respected developer and attracts the best talent for her company. The first time she coached one of her developers, instead of solving the problem herself, she felt like she'd let her team down. After all, they came to her because she was very smart, and they had a problem she could solve! In the past, she would have given them the answer, and they would have left smiling. At first, they struggled with her new approach. With time, though, she noticed that they came in ready to identify the issue and search themselves for the answers. McKinsie now has more time to focus on leading the business, and her team feels more confident to succeed.*

When leaders practice and see the outcomes of their coaching, they quickly overcome their perception of not having enough time. When they invest in developing others through coaching, they see the return of time come back to them and to their team.

"I'm Not Good at Relationships"

When I was coaching leaders and teams at Hewlett-Packard, the company was known for its engaging, high-performing culture in which everyone was encouraged to stretch and grow. I'll never forget Eddie, an engineer and manager. He told me that early in his career, Mike, a VP, took him aside and shared that while Eddie was very smart and promotable, Mike wouldn't want to go fishing with him. Eddie realized that Mike was sending Eddie a message about his people skills. So, Eddie signed up for all the advanced leadership programs, sought out feedback, and hired consultants to help him build each of his product research teams. Eddie became known as a leader with whom others liked to work. He took care of getting results *and* fostering strong relationships.

Eddie's a great example of the impact a growth mindset makes. Everyone on his teams believed they could learn, grow, and make mistakes along the way. He listened carefully to the feedback from Mike and recognized a gap in his leadership when it came to emotional intelligence and leading people. He sought out all the experiences, support, and learning he needed to grow that hat. Eddie continued to elicit and find value in the feedback he received from his teams—which is why they turned around and became productive, cohesive teams.

Like Eddie, you may be worried that you don't have the relationship skills necessary to coach. The good news is that every process of coaching builds skills that anchor relationships—and you can learn them. Recent studies affirm that when leaders coach, relationships, collaboration, and productivity (among other things) flourish.[13]

Learning to coach is like learning to swim. When you realize you can float, you're more willing to try the strokes that can take you from point A to B. It's a revelation, and the fear of drowning dissipates. Our biggest surprise in Leaders Who Coach was how many high-tech leaders loved learning to coach. The puzzle of how to communicate and move a coaching conversation forward was revealed. There was a roadmap they could follow (much like software development), and they helped others reach their destinations.

You, too, can learn the skills to coach people. Coaching will improve your ability to connect and work with everyone in your sphere of influence.

"I Work in a Top-Down Culture"

Until recently, "command-and-control" was the most common style of leadership in US culture. It's how many of us were mentored, and we naturally imitate that style, especially if we believe it's successful. Typically, the beliefs of a top-down culture are:

- I'm the manager, and I make the rules.
- I'm the source of knowledge and solutions.
- No news from me is good news. Screw up, and I'll tell you.
- Respect me, no matter what.
- I talk, and you listen.

These beliefs can discourage leaders from coaching because they imply that only the leaders are entrusted with the power of knowing and deciding. They tend to shut down autonomy and create a dependence on the leader for all solutions. Such a culture doesn't encourage innovation. During this titanic shift in our workplaces to less available talent and more need for organizations to adapt, these beliefs can stall your organization.

However, even in workplaces like the military, where command-and-control is an essential ingredient for success, collaboration and coaching are encouraged. My father, who graduated from West Point and fought in two wars, and my brothers, who fought in Vietnam, have said that the best commanders trusted the experience and perspective of their troops to collaborate on the best approach, even during war. Young officers were rapidly promoted, and results, not age or experience, were respected. There's a saying: "You're only as good as your sergeant major." My father encouraged his leadership to challenge him. He knew that ultimately their lives and his credibility were on the line, and he didn't have all the answers. Even in work cultures that require their team to follow orders, leaders can be encouraged to be humble and elicit the best ideas from others.

What You Believe Is Essential to Your Leadership and Coaching

Our mindsets are not wholly genetic or wired into our way of doing things. They are primarily developed by our environments; that which gets rewarded creates our beliefs and behaviors. For example, when we focus too much on success, we inhibit risk-taking and impede learning.

We move too quickly and tend to solve the wrong problems. Coaching intentionally slows down decision-making, so we can address the right issues and look at the best answers. In coaching, we embrace a growth mindset and the belief that no matter how capable you are, you can always improve through effort and practice.

So, does that mean everyone can improve and meet our standards? No, a person's values, motivation, and experience also determine whether they will grow. Coaching isn't a substitute for your responsibility to assess whether you have the right people on the bus or if a person's behavior and values prevent them from being successful on your bus.

These four beliefs support the development of leaders who coach in a work culture:

1. Everyone on the team has strengths and brings value to the whole.
2. We're all capable of improving and learning.
3. My role as a leader and manager is to pool our resources to collectively make the best decisions.
4. I'll empower you to make decisions and own solutions that support our mission and your development.

In today's knowledge economy, leaders are responding to constant change. If we're not agile, we can lose our competitive edge and our customers to someone who is. Finally, new generations entering our workforce don't tend to respond well to a command-and-control approach; instead, they seek collaboration and growth.

There are many reasons why you might choose not to coach. However, I challenge you to consider the impact on you, your team, and your organization if you do.

NEXT

- Review the values and beliefs underlying coaching. With which ones do you identify? What others are more challenging for you?

- Choose three values that you want to remind yourself about as you go through your day. Write these on a sticky note, then place it somewhere you'll be sure to see it. Read it every day and reflect on these values when you're preparing for a meeting or a communication with someone.
- Find a way to challenge the time objection to coaching. Try small moments where you listen and ask coaching questions to help someone. How much time did that take, and how was it helpful?

5

PRESENCE: SHOW UP AS A LEADER WHO COACHES

"Presence is a state of awareness, in the moment, characterized by the felt experience of timelessness, connectedness, and a larger truth."

—Doug Silsbee

AS A LEADER, you've learned to show up. When and how you show up can vary dramatically. Good leaders are authentic and bring their best selves for *each* purpose. How do you show up when you're delivering bad news? As Napoleon once said, the role of a leader is to "define reality and then give hope." How do you show up when you're announcing a new vision or change? What about when you're congratulating others or discussing an illness or challenging event? When do you put aside anger and negativity to lead calmly, and when do you let others know that you're deeply disappointed about their behavior? There isn't any formula because you're managing yourself as much as you're reading others and the situation. You're continually asking, "What's my purpose or goal here?"

There is an oft-quoted saying, "Leaders bring the weather." The impact of how leaders establish a vibe or atmosphere for others is real. We experience it every day. In coaching, we call showing up as a leader who coaches *presence*. This chapter is about how your behavior and intention can create presence. Presence is a quality that communicates to others that you're all there physically and psychologically; you're tuned in to the present. You're able to listen carefully, ignore distractions, and help the other person focus on themselves. The good news is that you have this ability in your repertoire. As you read through this chapter, reflect on how others have been present for you as they created the space for you to grow and learn.

Prepare Yourself to Show Up

The first step in creating presence is to prepare yourself. What's the buzz inside of you before you step forward? What are you anticipating? What feelings do you have as you prepare for the meeting or interaction? What emotions and priorities are crowding your thoughts? What story are you telling yourself about the next interaction? How can you let go of the story and stay focused on what and who is right in front of you? Rebecca discovered that simply focusing can be enough to establish presence.

I wasn't looking forward to my 1-2-1 with Meaghan. She tended to be scattered, and I found it challenging to feel helpful. I took a deep breath and focused on why I was coaching instead of telling. I realized that my frustration was about moving quickly. What I really wanted was to help Meaghan to be successful. I believed she was capable and motivated; I just wasn't sure she believed it. I arranged our chairs at my small table, so they faced each other and invited her to sit as I welcomed her.

"Hi, Meaghan—great to see you again." I took a deep breath. "This 1-2-1 is your meeting, and my goal is to support you and coach you about any issue or goal you feel is important." I paused and smiled. "So, what's up for you today, and what do you want our focus to be?"

Meaghan surprised me by jumping right in. "Well, I'm really struggling with prioritizing my projects. I make progress on one, and then someone calls me about the status of another. Sometimes I feel like I'm playing whack-a-mole and not getting anywhere. I know it's affecting my results, and I'd love some help."

Meaghan's willingness to talk about a major issue touched me. "I know how that feels, and it's not fun. I get the sense that prioritizing has really been challenging for you for some time now, and you're concerned about whether you're progressing on your goals. I appreciate you bringing this up, and I'm happy to coach you."

Meaghan nodded and smiled slightly. I think my open body language and clear focus on what was important to her helped her to take the leap. She knew I was there for her. We had a place to start and someplace to go, and I could begin to coach.

First Steps to Presence

Presence is first becoming clear on your purpose and mindset before going into communication with the other person. You set the tone by settling yourself and reviewing what you need to let go of to serve as a coach. You put aside your feelings and problems, so you can focus on what's important to the person or team in front of you. Then you can channel your focus into how to show up. As you review the qualities and behaviors of showing up, ask yourself which qualities are natural for you and which require more intention or focus on being with others.

Actively Show Acceptance and Support

No one will want to be coached if they don't feel accepted. When people feel accepted, they feel freer to explore. They aren't worried about making mistakes or being wrong. The coaching mindset is essential. Acceptance starts with a positive body posture and great listening skills. We aren't judging or giving direction. We simply become a way for others to hear themselves and see what's true for them.

Support is about being open, helpful, and encouraging. When we encourage others and listen to them, we help them open doors to discover who they are and where they want to go. Together, accepting and supporting others leads to trust, and trust is the bedrock of coaching. To be coached, your team needs to feel safe, so they can explore their emotions and thoughts, decide what they want, identify what's getting in their way, and figure out how they can solve it. They want to feel psychologically safe. *After all,* they think, *I might screw up or be seen as not capable.*

One natural challenge for leaders to be perceived as nonjudgmental is the inherent power of leading. For example, as a leader, you evaluate and give feedback to others. Your team is very conscious of what you think and believe because they want to be well regarded by their leader. Isn't that true for you when you think about your leader? You can't erase that dynamic totally, but you can establish your coaching presence by intentionally focusing on understanding and supporting the other person. The coaching skills we review in chapter 7 help to build trust with the person you're coaching.

Taking the time to be present for another person means showing them that their agenda and goals are paramount. Here are some guidelines leaders in our program identify as accepting and supportive:

- Be open and attentive in your body language.
- Nod and encourage.
- Work to see the other person's point of view.
- Reflect the others' emotions.
- Listen actively and intently.

Being accepting and supportive communicates that you're invested in the conversation and are an advocate for the other person's success.

Facilitate Focus

Coaching requires focus—and continuous refocus. One of the leaders from our program summed up what it means to focus:

> *I find that now when I meet with people in my office, I turn off my computer and my phone. I sit facing the person, and I leave behind whatever I was doing to have this conversation and determine if this is a coachable moment. I've been amazed at the result. People are more animated. They offer more about what they need or want. They're willing to explore when I ask coaching questions, and what's more surprising is that the interaction doesn't seem to take the time it did in the past. It's like anything else: When I focus, they focus—and we move forward.*

Focus isn't easy in this day of constant social media and electronic interruptions. Yet it's essential if teams and businesses are to evolve. When you make the transition to a coaching conversation, give yourself a moment to pause and breathe. You put space between your previous task and the coaching conversation ahead of you. Imagine that it's a different part of your brain, and you're awakening it to employ your coaching skills. You take off the other leadership hat that requires you to shoulder the load and have all the answers.

Here's what leaders who've been through our coaching program identify as the key ways to focus:

- Put aside distractions and identify the purpose of the conversation.
- Attend with your body—lean in; make appropriate eye contact.
- Refuse to go down rabbit holes that aren't essential to the topic or to the goals identified.
- Acknowledge new directions taken by the person you're coaching.
- Check—and recheck—whether the person being coached feels like you're on the right track.

Be Committed

Being present also means being committed to:

- The growth of others
- Following through
- Making time and refraining from jumping in and adding too much value

Often, commitment means providing time, resources, encouragement, and follow-through. By demonstrating these behaviors when you coach, you're showing others that they're important to you. In coaching, as in leadership, commitment inspires trust and engagement in others. What you model, others tend to emulate. As a committed leader, here's how you can demonstrate commitment when you coach:

- Make time for your 1-2-1s and coaching meetings—and keep them.
- Follow through on your agreements.
- Remember the topics and commitments of the people you coach.
- Be patient as you coach—everyone has their own timing. The coaching process supports forward movement, but it's their movement, not yours.

Stay Curious

Curiosity is both a mindset and a set of behaviors in coaching. When you're truly curious about the other person's issue, you'll come across as objective and without an agenda. It seems like a contradiction; I know. How can you want to know without projecting your own needs? Curiosity is about being inquisitive in a way that supports the person being coached and their goals. You don't expect a particular answer, and you're open to listening to however that person responds. As a leader, you want to know how the organization's performing and what the person's doing to contribute. However, the need to know is off the table when you coach. Those conversations are important for you to initiate at another time.

Remember the coach approach: you aren't asking because you need to know for your purposes; you're asking because you want to illuminate what the person really wants, how they got here, and what it will take to get there. A curious mind, without judgment, helps the other person see what's true and uncovers many aspects of themselves and situations that have been hidden. Curiosity also unleashes creative and innovative thinking that someone hasn't tapped into as they struggle with deciding what they should do. At the very least, when you're curious, you send the message to the person you're coaching that you're truly interested in and value what they say and how they feel. In chapter 7, I describe how coaching questions are different from other questions and how they can help you frame curiosity into open-ended inquiry. Leaders define curiosity as *presence* with the following behaviors:

- Selflessness
- Exploration
- Tentativeness and being nonjudgmental
- Not expecting a specific answer

How do you show up when you have your coaching hat on? You're receptive, focused, curious, and committed to supporting others' goals and development. Without saying anything, your coaching presence creates an open atmosphere for others to explore what's possible and then act. Many leaders have described being present as liberating. You're liberated from knowing. Todd Musselman, a Vistage speaker, describes presence as "the portal to being everything as a human." How we show up in a conversation is an opportunity to change the moment and be with the other person if we're willing.

The ability to be present is valued throughout the world. For example, in Africa, when people meet, they greet each other with the word *saubona*, which literally means "I see you." More than a greeting, *saubona* communicates that "I recognize your worth and dignity." When we recognize one another in that way, anything's possible.

NEXT

- How do you respond when others are present in the ways described in this chapter?
- What aspects of presence are most comfortable for you to show: acceptance, support, commitment, curiosity, or focus? How do you demonstrate those qualities?
- Which of these are most challenging for you, and what would you like to improve?
- At the next meeting with your team, intentionally focus on one way to be present that's most natural for you. Then, intentionally focus on the one that's most challenging.

6

WHEN YOU COACH, EVERYONE IS VULNERABLE

"Effective listening involves not only tuning in to others but tuning in to ourselves. Listening carefully to what we say and how we say it can teach us an immense amount about ourselves."

—Madelyn Burley-Allen

WHEN LEADERS ACCEPT the possibility that they don't know and others do, they're willing to be vulnerable. By definition, being vulnerable means we're uncomfortable because we're taking a risk. According to researcher and thought leader Brené Brown, being vulnerable means opening up to uncertainty, risk, and emotional exposure. Only then can we unleash the genius underneath. For example, leaders recognize that there are no guarantees in sustaining or growing their business.

Paradoxically, when leaders acknowledge the reality of not knowing or not being able to predict, they're also able to accelerate new ideas for growth and innovation.

The ongoing uncertainty of the COVID-19 epidemic has accelerated our willingness to be vulnerable. Acknowledging that reality to others is an example of being vulnerable. It's being willing to say, "I don't know. I can't predict." Without vulnerability, there's no courage to move forward. Without vulnerability, there's no innovation. You must be willing to risk failure and make mistakes to develop resilience. The mantra of an entrepreneur is often, "Fail often, fail cheap, fail early." Learn from how you fail and build better.

Vulnerability is inherent in the coaching relationship. The leader coaching and the person(s) being coached are stepping into the unknown and are willing to acknowledge that they need help or don't have all the answers. However, there are many myths that prevent us from embracing vulnerability as a strength. Let's examine three of the most common.

Vulnerability Myth 1: *Being vulnerable feels like weakness, and the leader projects this.* We tell ourselves that when we let others know we're uncertain or don't have the answers, their trust in our leadership will wane. We believe that an armor through which others can't see is the best way to inspire others to follow us. History, however, is filled with staggering examples of just the opposite. For venerated leaders like Abraham Lincoln and Oprah Winfrey, sharing uncertainty and challenges is perceived as a strength and inspires trust in others. As Brené Brown tells us, "Daring is not saying 'I'm willing to risk failure.' Daring is I know I will eventually fall, and I'm still all in."[14]

Also, the lack of transparency and the psychological armor that can't be pierced results in an inability to learn. We refuse to risk, and we don't grow. We don't believe others can change. We keep ourselves, our team, and our business in a box, but it's a box that doesn't reflect the reality of a changing world. Stepping into an ambiguous world takes courage. The rate of change in our world is exponentially accelerating; if we don't have the courage to leave our ego behind, we'll be left behind. When you coach, you practice being vulnerable, and practice becomes presence.

Vulnerability isn't just about coaching; it's part of cultivating humility in your leadership. According to Jim Collins, the author of *Good to Great*,[15] who studied the highest level of effective leaders, being both resolute and humble are the qualities of leaders who build great companies. Humble leaders give others credit, develop others to succeed them, and seek the input of others to make the best decisions.

Vulnerability Myth 2: *Being vulnerable means spewing our feelings and thoughts without purpose.* Good leaders maintain boundaries. They share emotions, experiences, and insights at the right time. For example, leaders sharing important emotions can result in emotional contagion. When shared indiscriminately, this can damage morale or cause confusion. Sharing emotions thoughtfully, on the other hand, can spread hope, positivity, and encouragement.

> *Justin heard Melinda, one of his team members, struggling with a complex problem. Inside, he was struggling as well because he didn't have the solution, and he thought he should. Finally, he divulged that he, too, was stymied about the best way to approach the issue.*
>
> *"I'll be honest, Melinda. This would be a tough problem for me as well." He noticed that Melinda seemed to relax. She wasn't being judged. He then said, "I'd like to hear more of your ideas about what would make this work better. I'll bet with your experience, you have many."*

Vulnerability Myth 3: *We won't know how to deal with the emotions that may come with feeling vulnerable.* "I'm not a counselor, after all," one leader remarked. As you'll hear throughout this book, our emotions are essential for decision-making, dealing with stress, and understanding what people want. While the *name it to tame it* mantra of emotional intelligence seems counterintuitive, it allows the brain to let go and understand the meaning of emotions. In coaching, we first hear how others are feeling, and then we help them name it and choose how to manage it. Leaders discover very quickly that emotions show up and often dissipate as the person better understands what they want. Emotions tend to be more powerful when they're unspoken or hidden.

When you coach as a leader, you're being vulnerable. You're choosing to say, "I don't have all the answers." When you begin to coach, you're choosing to learn a new way to lead. It's like any other skill you've learned. You'll make mistakes. You won't be perfect. When you coach, you're also choosing to be open to feelings and experiences that are very different than your own. That's what Justin did. He modeled for Melinda that it was okay to question and struggle. By doing so, he also risked feeling more connected, empathetic, and understanding.

When Melinda shared her struggles, she chose to be vulnerable with her boss. She was willing to say, "I don't know, but I want to discover a better way. I trust that you'll accept me, with all my uncertainty, for who I am." She trusted that Justin wouldn't see her indecision, doubts, or need for help as inadequacy. Successful coaching is built on trust.

The Do-Over

Laura was a recently promoted leader whose team had grown rapidly from two to eight members in the last six months. She was a leader who saw the power of coaching and looked for opportunities to coach every day. She was alarmed that one of her new team members, Lucas, was working long hours and starting to show up tired and without his usual positive attitude. What was causing him to work so many hours? she wondered. At the end of the day, Laura decided to visit Lucas and find out more.

From the beginning, Lucas kept looking at his watch. He patiently answered Laura's questions about his workload and how he felt, but he never offered his agenda or needs, and the meeting ended with no outcome for either of them. Laura scratched her head. What could she have done differently?

When Laura asked to be coached on her coaching, we discovered that her concern about Lucas came from her own painful experience with burnout early in her career. She feared that Lucas might not last in his role if he kept up the long hours. We talked about whether it would be appropriate for her to tell Lucas about her experience as a way to own her observation and increase trust.

> *Although Laura was uncomfortable being vulnerable by sharing, she was willing to experiment with a do-over to see if she and Lucas could connect differently about the experience. Rather than wait until Friday, she opted to have a meeting earlier in the week to share her experiences and concern.*
>
> *Lucas's response was immediate. He not only revealed that he was overwhelmed in his role, but he also requested help in setting new goals for himself. By disclosing her experience and related concerns, Laura had invited Lucas to do the same.*

Let's be clear: These moments of vulnerability, whether small or large, can make coaching uncomfortable. But in that vulnerability are deep opportunities for everyone to connect, innovate, and grow the organization.

NEXT

- Reflect on times when you felt vulnerable and how it led to growth.
- Identify moments to share when you don't know something or don't have the answers. Invite others to help or share.
- When was the last time you shared feelings about feeling sad, fearful, or unsure? What was the outcome?

7

THREE COACHING SKILLS TO GET YOU THERE

"Questions are really powerful in creating safety—
they indicate to someone that you actually want to hear their voice."

—Amy Edmondson

THE FIRST CHAPTERS of this book focused on cultivating a coach approach mindset and an understanding of who you need to be to coach your team members effectively. Without that mindset, coaching skills will likely fall flat and not be successful. Great coaching requires all of you. Now you're ready to learn how and what you must do to coach.

The *how* of coaching consists of skills that set the groundwork for building trust, understanding the other person, and paving the way forward. This chapter will help you understand three essential skills to help others. When you get down to it, these coaching skills are also powerful tools for communication and collaboration. When leaders attend our program, they often exclaim how vital coaching skills are for effective everyday leadership.

You use many of these skills already, and some of them may feel natural the very moment you try them on. Others will feel like ill-fitting clothes until you move around in them and discover that you can wear them well. Then you wear these skills to help the person you're coaching to move to the destination they've identified. As you read this chapter, reflect on the times you've used these skills, as well as times you wish you had.

In our program, leaders learn to coach by coaching and being coached multiple times. They're being coached by their fellow coaching novices, all using the coach approach, skills, and process described in this book. At the end of the program, participants share that they've received significant insights from being coached by other newly developed leaders who coach. They discover that, like any competency—from making piecrusts to reading profit-and-loss statements—you can only become a leader who coaches when you commit to practicing.

This chapter describes the three essential coaching skills: listening, asking coaching questions, and encouraging. While there are additional coaching skills, these are the building blocks necessary for you to coach. In coaching, we listen to words, body language, intent, and the story behind the story. Coaching questions are intentionally open-ended and without a solution attached for the purpose of helping others focus and discover. We encourage others when we build on strengths, notice what went well, and provide supportive feedback. All these skills are designed to invite others to explore, focus, and have the courage to try something new or develop differently.

LISTENING: A Coach's Most Valuable Skill

We hear it all the time. Listening is the most valued skill in our workplaces. We all remember when someone listened to us deeply, and we experienced the magic of being understood. They got us! Few of us excel at it because, in our culture, we tend to reward telling or being the smartest person in the room.[16] Yet the best salespeople tend to be great listeners, and leaders who seek first to understand multiple perspectives make better decisions.

As described in chapter 5, one way we listen is by being present. We shut out all distractions inside and outside and focus on the other person. In coaching, we listen actively, verbally reflecting back what we think others mean. Listening is *the* most important coaching skill, and it takes intentional effort. Here are three reasons why listening actively is foundational to coaching.

First, listening allows you to enter into and accept the world of the other person. It doesn't matter if you agree or disagree when you're listening actively. Your role is to accurately understand what the other person wants and needs. It's also important for you to know where your perceptions may differ from theirs so you don't make assumptions.

Second, listening builds the foundation of trust. When the other person knows that you understand not only what they're saying (the content) but also why they're saying it (their intent), they're more willing to open up and explore new options. They're more willing to explore hard topics. They're more willing to take risks and be challenged. It's that simple.

Third, listening can lead to change. A good listener becomes a mirror through which the other person can hear and see themselves. They can be transformed when they hear their own emotions, perceptions, and experiences voiced by someone else. They may feel affirmed and often take that opportunity to add, subtract, or even challenge their thinking. It's hard to forget the experience of being listened to well.

It's just as important to know when you're *not* listening. You're not listening when you:

- **Listen selectively for your agenda.** Lingering in the front or back of most leaders' minds is the filter of hearing everything through their mission and goals. When you use those filters, it becomes about *your* agenda, not the other person's goals. That's when you start making assumptions and giving advice.

- **Pretend to listen.** You may be nodding and quiet, but your brain isn't present to what the person's saying. Your mind is like a monkey, moving quickly from one topic to another, and what the other person's saying is lost.

- **Judge**. When you're busy hearing what's right and wrong, good and bad, smart and incompetent, etc., you create walls that block the other person's perspective. You only hear your judgments. Your natural filters are always present, but it's the degree to which you assign and hold on to your judgment of the other person's ideas, feelings, and value that impacts your ability to truly connect. When you adopt the role of critical leader, it's only a matter of time before you communicate your judgment, directly or indirectly.

- **Are distracted**. Unfortunately, we're easily sidetracked from paying attention to this moment, this person. Our electronic extensions further trigger our brains to jerk and attend to the next ping, sound, or intrusion. Put them aside. Leaders tell us one of the first things they learn when they coach is to turn off their inner and outer distractions. Contrary to the belief that multitasking gets more done, our brains simply can't do this efficiently. Distractions undermine your time with others and often will prolong the meeting with the person with whom you're coaching.

Tips for Listening Well

Silence the voices in your head. Being human means we're constantly interpreting the world. We create unique realities through our filters and stories. We each have a special pair of prescription glasses through which we see the world. While this can be beautiful, our different glasses can also be incredibly challenging. Each day we have opportunities to communicate with one another clearly so that we can understand and be understood. Listening helps bridge that space, and the first step is listening to yourself. What are you telling yourself about the person and the story unfolding before you? What assumptions, beliefs, and judgments emerge?

While you may not be able to entirely turn off your stories, you can turn them down. First, raise your awareness. Have you veered off the listening path back to your internal world? When you notice this, gently turn your attention back to the other person. Resist thinking that you know what they mean. Instead, adopt a mindset of inquiry and curiosity.

Set the stage for listening. Position yourself and create an environment that's inviting and open to exploring and having a coaching conversation. Whether you're walking together or sitting down, these tips can help set the stage for communicating well together.

- Turn off all outside distractions.
- Prepare yourself—let go of thoughts and take a few deep breaths.
- Face the speaker (unless walking).
- Maintain friendly eye contact (if culturally appropriate).
- Lean forward and be open in your posture (if culturally appropriate).
- Nod or make encouraging sounds.

Remember to WAIT. WAIT is a reminder to ask yourself, "Why Am I Talking?" If what you're saying is not related to understanding what the other person wants or is saying, then WAIT. When you're coaching someone, the conversation is about them, not you. Engage with them by listening.

Brent, a newly promoted leader, was feeling frustrated when one of his direct reports, Lora, didn't volunteer for challenging assignments. Lora had told him that she wanted a promotion. He championed her growth with enthusiasm by offering a variety of projects that could lead to another role. However, Lora never stepped up to take the offer. In fact, her approach to performance seemed to be "just tell me how you want this project done, and I'll complete it." Brent realized that he needed to stop talking about new opportunities and find out how Lora was really feeling about learning and growing.

"Lora, I hear that you want to go to the next level, but I also notice that doing different projects is uncomfortable for you. For example, you seem to love writing reports, but you don't want to write a marketing plan for us. I'd like to hear more about what the difference is for you."

Lora shifted her attention, and Brent noticed she was looking down instead of looking at the Zoom camera. Finally, she said, "No, I'm definitely not comfortable writing a marketing plan. I've never done it before. I'm afraid. I don't want to make mistakes, and I don't feel confident that I won't screw up if I write something I've never written before."

Brent felt as though a wall between them had been removed. He didn't try to talk her out of her feelings. "Thanks for letting me know, Lora. It seems that when you feel confident about doing a good job, you're eager to tackle a project. I understand—I want to be successful at what I do too. So, what stops you from trying new things is feeling like you won't be successful, and you don't want to risk it."

Lora nodded, then added, "I feel that if I just stick with what I know I do well, I'll be okay."

Brent's willingness to listen actively to Lora and meet her where she was created a genuine conversation about what was holding Lora back. It was the first time they'd ever discussed why Lora avoided taking on projects. It was a milestone in their relationship.

Attend to and listen with all of you. At least 70 percent of all communication is nonverbal. It's even more important to pay attention to how others are communicating and listen to the messages contained within their tone of voice, facial expression, body language, etc. Our brains are wired to intuitively perceive the nonverbal if only we pay attention.

Key questions to ask yourself:

- What emotions might this person's facial expression or tone of voice be expressing?
- How do I sense their energy (energized, excited, depleted, withdrawn, etc.)?
- What impact does the person's nonverbal behavior have on me? Do I feel sad or frustrated when I hear their story?

- Am I feeling confused? Do their nonverbal and verbal messages send a mixed message?

Since the meaning of nonverbal behaviors can vary greatly from culture to culture and person to person, be tentative when you reflect what you're hearing. Many tears have fallen that stemmed from frustration and anger, not sadness.

I was once referred to Gina, a senior woman manager who'd been given feedback that she was too emotional because she was sometimes tearful when she communicated with others. Gina and I both acknowledged that gender bias may have been a factor in the feedback. Then we explored what was behind her emotion. We first identified that she was most likely to be tearful at leadership team meetings. As she remembered those meetings, she began to tear up.

"I notice you're tearing up right now. What's going on?" I asked.

"I'm angry," she stated. "My department is continually slighted when others are recognized. Our contribution is huge."

Our conversation shifted dramatically to what she wanted others to know (besides tears) and what was holding her back from sharing with her peers.

We don't always know what someone else's nonverbal behaviors mean to them. There's no nonverbal dictionary to accurately tell us. When we take a moment to listen actively to what we see, it can lead to an amazing discovery of what's true for others.

How to Listen Actively to Understand

When you're coaching, how can you know that what you think you're hearing is accurate? You can only truly know if you share what you're hearing. The skill of active listening seems like a paradox because you're both talking and listening. However, active listening is the key to creating a shared understanding of the world with the person you're coaching. Leaders can also listen actively to teams, summarizing the ideas or themes being expressed by the whole team. As a leader who coaches, you silence your voice and actively engage to ensure that what you're receiving is accurate. First, tune in to the different layers of communication and then share what you're hearing.

Three Layers of Verbal Communication

- **Content**: *What are they saying?* This is the basic level of listening. We're simply hearing the content. This level of listening seeks to understand what may seem obvious in a sequence of events or the first level of meaning. What happened, and how did that affect them? When the person hears what they said, they often correct themselves, add more clarification, or fill in an important point.
- **Intent/Meaning:** *What do they mean?* In this layer, we're trying to understand the person's intent or meaning behind what they're saying. These messages may be stated or implied. The intent is often more important and differs from the content. You might ask yourself, "What's the intent behind them sharing this story? What's the overall meaning of them bringing this issue to me?"
- **Emotions**: *How do they feel?* When we listen with our heart, we notice the emotions inherent in someone's story, even if we don't hear them said directly. Tone of voice is another powerful indicator of what someone's feeling. I've noticed that when I prompt leaders to stop and notice what they're hearing, they can reflect the unsaid, deeper meaning of the communication.

At the beginning of a coaching conversation, listening for content is often appropriate. The leader as coach is simply trying to understand the context of the situation and the other person's perspective. However, as the coaching conversation progresses, listening actively to meaning and emotions helps uncover what's most important to the person and why. This data enables the person being coached to unearth their wants and goals.

Think back to a recent conversation you've had with someone about something important to them. Imagine that you have an opportunity to reflect back to them the essence, or meaning, of what they said. How might the conversation have changed if you'd taken the time to do so?

Early in my career, I worked with a nursing team who was communicating with one another disrespectfully. It was unusual for them to do so, and their manager was puzzled and concerned. When I first met with them, I thought the problem was their lack of communication skills. Then I realized they could've taught a course in communication skills—they all had master's degrees. I felt stymied and ineffectual. It wasn't a good feeling.

I decided to get over myself, ask them a different question, and just listen. "I know you have tough jobs. I also know you've been doing this for a while and love being part of Intensive Care. Whatever your reason is for behaving toward one another the way you are right now, I'm going to assume it's a good reason. You're good people. Are you willing to talk about what's really bothering you?"

There was silence, and then one by one, they started to speak up. "I'm scared. There are too many people dying on this unit, and I don't understand why."

Someone else spoke up. "Me too. I'm pregnant. Can I catch what these patients have?" The conversation turned from hostility to shared understanding. I never referred to the disrespectful behavior that was the original focus of my consultation. We were addressing the core issue. The whole conversation became about the *why* of their behavior.

Empathetic Listening—A Powerful Coaching Skill

If ever there was a time for us to listen, it's now. If ever there was a time for empathy, it's today. The grief, anguish, anger, and accelerated change during the COVID-19 pandemic and the social change we're experiencing in and outside the workplace require leaders to connect emotionally. Our collective experiences will endure throughout our lives. Whether we're alike or different, listening empathetically communicates that we care and want to understand. It's also key for bridging gaps and creating trust.

Empathetic listening is an essential coaching tool. When we coach, we connect to reflect others' emotions, beliefs, and perceptions. Others see and hear themselves anew, and emotions help clarify situations and motivate them to move forward. Integrating emotions into our listening, without judgment, helps reveal all the data and creates a safe place to explore.

How do we define *empathy*? Empathy is demonstrating that we care about and understand what someone's feeling inside or how they're seeing the world. It's inherent in listening actively. You can express empathy in different ways by accessing different parts of your brain. Several studies distinguish between different components of empathy.[17]

- **Perspective Taking** uses our cognitive brain when we *infer* how others are feeling and thinking to understand their perspective. The act of reflecting another person's perspective is inherent when you listen during coaching.
- **Empathetic Concern** is the expression of compassion for the other person. We care and feel *for* the other person. Concern is particularly important when others' feelings are difficult and self-limiting. However, it's fine to express concern only when it's authentic for you. We may not know exactly what it's like to lose a child or have cancer, or experience discrimination. We can connect, however, with the themes of loss and rejection.

It turns out that it's usually not enough to imagine what the person's feeling; we need to express what we're hearing. We call this *empathetic paraphrasing*. Studies show that when leaders engage in reflecting back the emotions they hear, others actually see leaders as more empathetic.[18] Furthermore, these studies confirm that empathetic listening by leaders results in positive outcomes for employee engagement, performance, and retention.[19] Expressing empathy is a muscle we can strengthen simply by tuning in to how the person perceives or feels about a situation. Employ the *name it to tame it* principle to help connect and clarify.

You also can help yourself and others find words for emotions by using a feeling wheel. (You'll find the Gottman Institute Feeling Wheel in Appendix B with instructions on how to use it and learn from it.) If you aren't accurate, the other person will let you know. They might say something like, "No, actually, I'm feeling pretty good about what I did. I think it's what happened next that I'm stewing about." The dynamic of empathetic concern naturally deepens the conversation.

Listening Actively in Action

- **Reflect, in their own words, what they're saying.**
  - I'm hearing two concerns: you'd like to know if you have a career path here, and you want feedback about how you can improve.
  - What's coming across right now is that you aren't feeling appreciated and want to know how to be successful here.
  - You seem to be saying that you're stuck and frustrated with other people's lack of response to your request for mentoring.
  - You feel excited about growing with this project, but you don't know where to begin.
- **Be tentative each time you listen actively, showing that you're attentive and open to correction**. When others hear themselves, they'll either get you back on their track, or they'll continue to add to your expressed understanding of the situation.
- **Interrupt to listen.** Interrupting to listen actively can help your interaction turn into a coaching conversation. You develop a stream of understanding. Interrupting to actively listen may seem contradictory to the notion of listening. We're taught that it's rude to interrupt. Indeed, if we interrupt to share our story or perception, it isn't listening.

In coaching, we interrupt to create a process of mutual understanding. So much communication can occur that we don't understand, and we can easily make erroneous assumptions. Let enough of the story be told before you interrupt to listen actively. Another challenge is that our ears are the most inefficient way to gather data. Our hearing is slow and restricted. Within even a minute, we've lost the opportunity to help others hear themselves, check out our understanding, or challenge them to go one step deeper in defining what's important to them. The time to interrupt is:

- When something important has been expressed, and you want to use the power of listening to affirm what they're saying
- When you're getting lost and can't keep track of the purpose, feelings, or content
- When they're repeating themselves and seem unfocused

If you're concerned about being rude, you can always ask permission to interrupt.

- "May I interrupt to make sure I'm understanding you?"
- "I may be getting confused; is this what you're saying?"

Whether you're aware of it or not, you use your listening skills every day—when you're listening to the marketplace for opportunities, listening and noticing when your team's morale has shifted, listening to communication go flat, or listening by reading the room. As a leader who coaches, listening is approximately 75 percent of what you do.

Finally, there are a few phrases that I recommend you *not* use when you're listening or empathizing as a coach:

- "I know how you feel . . ."
- "Yes, I understand (without saying what you understand from their perspective) . . ."
- "I've had that experience too . . . *blah, blah, blah.*"

In Appendix A, you'll find a series of phrases that will help you communicate that you're listening actively. Some of them, such as "I hear you saying . . ." or "It sounds like . . ." may seem trite because they're generic. Yet leaders in our program use them again and again, and because they're present, connected, and accurate, others hear them as genuine.

ASKING: The Power of Coaching Questions

Asking coach-like questions is a skill that transforms any conversation into one that discovers hidden jewels of insight, uncovers barriers, and challenges us—all at the same time. Coaching questions are unique because they don't have a solution embedded in them. At their core, coaching questions encourage others to reflect and open doors to rooms they didn't even know were there. They come from your curiosity and your goal to:

- invite creativity and new possibilities
- generate energy and forward movement
- surface beliefs and assumptions

In my experience, after leaders struggle to let go of their solutions and begin focusing on asking questions designed to help others think, reflect, and feel, they quickly grasp how to ask coaching questions. Think of coaching questions as tilling the soil by unearthing nuggets of motivations, beliefs, and goals. We turn over the ground to produce healthy solutions that will grow.

Effective coaching questions:

- tend to start with "what" or "how"
- almost never start with "why"
- raise the person's awareness of themselves and others
- emerge from the person's agenda and language
- discover rather than just ask for information

- open up possibilities and new awareness of thoughts, feelings, and motivations
- are content-free—opening doors rather than focusing on details that may or may not be important

One leader who was learning to coach had a hard time with coaching questions, so he decided to ask only three:

1. What do you want?
2. How important is that to you?
3. What's getting in your way?

He found that these questions yielded a good focus for others until he learned to vary his questions to fit more specifically to what the other person was saying.

Here are a few phrases that leaders who coach have generated:

- If this situation were resolved, what would that look like?
- What about this is important to you?
- What's working for you, and what needs to change?
- How are you getting in your own way of solving the problem?
- How is this issue currently affecting you?
- What about this situation do you feel strongly about?
- What's getting in the way of you reaching your goal?
- What ideas do you have about how to approach this situation?
- What else?

Notice how each of these questions can provide a doorway to another level of conversation and exploration. Asking "What else?" encourages others to simply say more—because often there's more to say.

Questions to Avoid

- Throughout this book, I've encouraged you to leave your solutions behind. Some questions scream, "I think you should . . ."—the solutions are embedded in the questions. For example, "Have you tried . . . ?" or "Can't you . . . ?" These types of questions usually come from your idea of what should happen and don't challenge the person to generate ideas and shape their own solutions.

- Avoid questions that can be answered with a yes or no. "Do you want to . . . ?" or "Have you considered . . . ?" or "Did you try . . . ?" These questions do not provide an opportunity for the person being coached in determining their own reasoning or thoughts. They can simply reply yes or no—and then the ball's back to you to direct the conversation.

- "Why" questions are rarely helpful in coaching because they tend to put people on the defensive. They imply blame. Also, they invite analysis and explanation rather than exploration and opening up. Finally, "why" questions are often an invitation to go down a rat hole, where the desired outcome plays second fiddle to details that may not be relevant.

When you begin coaching, you're bound to ask these kinds of dead-end questions. They're common in our work conversations. Not to worry—you'll have plenty of opportunities to ask the question in a different way, often in the next moment. On the other hand, great coaching questions help the person focus and peek around the corner to discover something they hadn't noticed was there.

After listening to Mike's goal of improving his confidence in his role, Teisha wondered out loud, "What would be different if you were confident?" Mike stopped and thought intently. He focused and imagined. "I wouldn't use filler words. I'd enter conversations with the team earlier rather than fade into the background." Teisha's question helped Mike begin to create a clear picture of what confidence in himself looked like.

With her coaching question, she was able to shift the conversation to something tangible he could see and practice.

If you're listening well and asking yourself what questions would help this person understand himself and the issue, then you can create your own coaching questions. With practice, they'll become natural. I suggest trying what most professional coaches do—write down generic or related questions before you coach. It only takes a few minutes. When I do that, my brain warms up to being curious and focused. I let go of having answers.

Coaching questions can also be magical ways to help others imagine what's possible and challenge them to see what's hidden. Deep within a coaching question is always the assumption that the person you're coaching has the ability to resolve, solve, or figure out what will work for them. Questions can also challenge the person to dig deep to envision new ways to act and think. Asking powerful questions and listening work together to facilitate effective coaching. I often say that for every coaching question you ask, meaningful listening should follow. In chapter 8, I'll share how coaching questions—asked at the right time—help the person you're coaching arrive at their action plan.

Encouraging

When leaders are asked to share a time when someone encouraged them and made a difference, their faces light up, and they share inspiring stories. There's no shortage of genuine gratitude for the person who encouraged them.

Yet many leaders don't see encouragement as a leadership strength. Even if they do, others who report to them often tell them they'd like more appreciation and encouragement. There are many reasons why leaders rarely share enough encouragement and appreciation. First, they don't acknowledge that they themselves need encouragement, and they assume that others are like them. Second, leaders assume that people know that they feel positive about them. Third, some leaders are so focused on results and time pressures that they don't focus on positively encouraging others. Studies find that the ratio of negative to positive feedback that motivates most people differs from culture to culture and person to person. In the US, the norm is one negative feedback to every three positive ones. The optimum ratio is 1:5.[20]

Individuals can also vary greatly in their need for encouragement. When employees feel genuinely valued for the specific ways they contribute, their engagement rises. They're more likely to stay, put discretionary energy into their work, and see their goals aligned with the goals of the organization.[21]

The role of encouragement in coaching is even more important. Coaching conversations often involve someone coming to you to tackle challenging situations. When we encourage as we coach, we acknowledge the challenge, and we express belief in the person's strengths and ability to stretch.

As a CFO of a nonprofit, Pat was known for supporting and giving credit to others for their many accomplishments. However, she felt unsure of how her leadership contributed to the team's success. "I want to be a better leader. How do I make a difference here?" she asked her CEO, Ted.

"Well, Pat, let's look at the way you managed the grants we just received. Our audit was perfect. What difference do you think that made to the team?"

Pat shrugged it off. "I was just doing my job. It wasn't a big deal."

Ted pushed on. "Actually, the team was relieved when the monies and dispersion went without a hitch. That wasn't just true of my grant, but of all the grants that you managed. The team trusts you, Pat, and so do I."

Pat was surprised and then beamed. "I didn't know," she said. "I guess that's the real area of growth for me. I'm going to ask others on the team for their positive feedback and stop assuming that I'm failing. Thanks for helping me see what I didn't."

Ted encouraged her again, saying, "I think that's a terrific idea, Pat. Let me know what you learn!"

As a leader who coaches, there are many opportunities to encourage others. If you're aware of the person's strengths or successes, you can share that knowledge in a way that helps them gain confidence for the path ahead. For example, you can provide specific feedback about how they're making progress, and you can notice the subtle differences that are showing up. You can high-five people when they're sharing a win. You should weave encouragement throughout your coaching as you do with listening. Effective encouragement is always authentic, and it requires the coach to stop and notice what to appreciate and encourage, such as openness, willingness to take risks, tenacity, etc. Encouragement in coaching is about encouraging the person, not the task, and it's specific. For example, "I know you'll be able to accomplish that project" versus "I believe your passion for this project will energize your team."

Encouragement motivates others to continue down arduous paths and provides another mirror for positive attributes people might not see or acknowledge.

There are many different ways to express encouragement during your coaching, such as:

- "Thanks for coming in; I know it's hard to ask for help on this project."
- "I appreciate how willing you are to reach out to people when you're stuck, and I'm happy to help."
- "Recognizing your misstep is an important step toward improving. I appreciate your candor."
- "I gave this project to you because I know how effectively you can lead a team on a new project. How can I support you?"
- "I really appreciate your ability to ask strategic questions as we navigate the changing COVID situation. It helps everyone focus. What strategic questions come to mind with your challenge?"

These three essential skills—listening, asking questions, and encouraging—can change your leadership conversations dramatically.

They build trust and relationships because your team feels included and valued. When you use these coaching skills, you're taking the coach approach to leading. They're not sufficient by themselves, however, to effectively coach. Coaching, as you recall, is about helping people move forward. To complete a journey with a destination, you need a roadmap. The *what* of coaching is what I call the roadmap, and it's the secret sauce that propels individuals and teams forward.

NEXT

- Assess your three coaching skills on a scale of one to five, with five being exceptionally strong. Which one is strongest for you? In what area would you like to improve?
- Check out Appendix A and choose one new way to listen actively. Plan to ask three coaching questions the next time you meet with someone. Notice what happens.
- Intentionally listen actively in team and individual conversations. Ask coaching questions with the intent of creating more exploration and deeper dialogue. Practice these skills with your family too.
- Practice encouragement every day. Be immediate, specific, and positive! It may feel foolish or as though you're going overboard, but rarely do I hear anyone say, "My leader is too encouraging." Make encouragement a habit, and it will become natural in your coaching as well.

8

THE ROADMAP FOR COACHING

"When we unpack our distal aspirations, we better appreciate, plan for, navigate the difficulties of getting from here to there."

—Emily Bacetis

WHEN I FIRST began developing leaders to coach, people from diverse industries enthusiastically endorsed our program: high tech, manufacturing, firefighters, etc. It took us a while to understand what worked so well for these diverse leaders when soft skill and people skill training often did not.

Leaders told us that *the roadmap* for coaching is what made a difference. Mirroring professional coaching models and competencies, we provided them with a clear path and specific skills that achieved results. Then they coached and were coached by other leaders. They experienced how coaching felt and worked for them. When they coached others, they saw the results of their coaching: others gained insights and walked away with a plan. They also grasped how coaching could impact behaviors and business results. Most importantly, they believed they could immediately leave the coaching program and engage in coaching as leaders. The coaching roadmap was a powerful guide to unleash the knowledge and innovation in each person and in their teams.

Miles directed a team of twenty-five software developers at a university. The technology was always changing and those who were programming every day were on top of those changes. Yet, they often came to Miles for help when they were stuck. Miles reflected, They have more knowledge and experience than I do with these new programs. What can I do to help empower them to solve problems themselves? *Following his coach training, he applied the coaching model to a group of three developers who were working on a problem together. They filed into his room, expecting him to answer their questions. Rather than default to the role of expert, Miles spent time listening and asking questions to help them zero in on the underlying challenge. Then he invited them to draw their solutions on the whiteboard. Finally, he challenged them to choose a path. The developers left not only knowing how to get past their software conundrum but also confident that they had the ability—together—to solve it. Miles used the coaching roadmap. Although they still came to him for help, they knew they had the answers, and he would coach them to discover what they were.*

This book's coaching roadmap for leaders is built on the same mindset and core competencies as professional coaching models. As I have made clear, leaders who coach must first believe that people are resourceful, whole, and have strengths they can use to reach goals and solve problems. Then they use the coaching skills to progress on the roadmap. The roadmap I share with you is a clear and purposeful sequence of steps that build on each other to guide your coaching and help the person being coached to reach their goals. It begins with affirming the desired outcome of the person being coached and then proceeds to help the person forge their path to change, improve, or become. In our program, leaders experience the roadmap both as a coach and as a person being coached. It's that experience that solidifies the belief that others will benefit when they put on their coaching hat. As the Canadian rapper Drake said, "Sometimes it's the journey that tells you a lot about your destination."

The roadmap I present in this book reflects the research and effectiveness of many other coaching models, such as those created by Sir John Whitmore (GROW) and the *5/5/5 Coaching Out of the Box* model. I call the roadmap in this book PASN. It's designed to do what it sounds like: ignite passion and inspire commitment to grow.

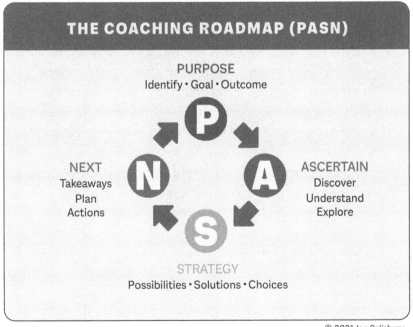

THE COACHING ROADMAP (PASN)

PURPOSE
Identify · Goal · Outcome

NEXT
Takeaways
Plan
Actions

ASCERTAIN
Discover
Understand
Explore

STRATEGY
Possibilities · Solutions · Choices

© 2021 Jan Salisbury

Purpose

Every successful coaching conversation starts with answering this question: What is the purpose of our conversation? Why are we here, and what outcome do you want from this conversation? What are your intentions? Sometimes the person you're coaching doesn't know exactly why they are there, and starting with their purpose helps them focus. In this stage, your role as a coach is to help them paint a vision of where they want to go. The *Purpose* phase can be used in many ways:

- Identify intentions and goals
- Understand what they want to change
- Become a reference point for where you began and a benchmark to determine if you've accomplished what was intended
- Clarify when the purpose is a moving target—coaching can start with one purpose and end up landing on another.

One of my colleagues is fond of saying, "If the meeting you're walking into doesn't have a purpose, turn around and attend a meeting that does." In other words, when you coach, begin with the other person's intention for the meeting or conversation. Even if you're coaching for only a few minutes, the *Purpose* stage of coaching is essential to providing direction and expectations. In fact, research on coach effectiveness affirms that agreement on the goals and purpose at the beginning of coaching is key to determining the effectiveness of coaching, especially when those goals are related to one's core values and sense of self.[22]

For example, when someone comes to tell you their story, or in some cases to vent, stop and ask one of the following questions:

- How can I help?
- When you walk out of here, what would you like to have accomplished?
- How might I help you with this issue?
- What outcome would you like from our time today?
- What's on your mind?

These types of coaching questions help the person become centered and focused, and they help you know if coaching is appropriate. People often don't know what they want, but when you listen and reflect on what they say, they figure it out. The questions also help you, the coach, stay focused on meeting the person's needs.

Sometimes there are competing goals: "I want to improve my communication skills, and I want to have more of a life." Or "I'm not sure. I just want to minimize the conflict with my co-worker." Reiterating their goals and clarifying which one they want to focus on the most can jumpstart the journey.

Starting your coaching journey with *Purpose* also helps you—as the coach—create a benchmark for assessing whether or not the coaching was successful. If you started with a focus on having "more of a life," you could circle back to see if the person made progress on that goal. You can also help others create time-limited purposes when your time to talk is limited. You might say, "In the time we have available, what would you like to achieve in this conversation?"

In coaching, we place the importance on what's most meaningful for the person we're coaching. Once they're clear about where they're going, we can help them explore how, when, etc. When *they* choose the mountain to climb, your role is to skillfully help them decide how to climb it. What's the best path? What will get in the way? How can they best prepare? Along the way, as you both uncover new streams and paths, they may realize they're on the wrong path or even going to the wrong destination. Coaching is a journey, and a straight path without deviation is the exception, not the norm. At each junction, there's a choice. As a coach, you ask, "How can I help you choose what's best and what's next for you?" The *Purpose* stage is just a beginning, and you may find yourself returning to it when the path changes.

Mia had just become a team leader responsible for six direct reports. It didn't take her long to realize that the previous manager had never met individually with the team and only met as a group once a month. No wonder, she thought to herself, that people aren't motivated or aligned about where they were going! Every day was about reacting to a problem.

Her first task was to begin regular meetings. She realized her team was not used to coaching, so she explained that these 1-2-1 meetings were their time to focus on issues and development. Here's how one of her meetings went:

Mia: Hi, Drew. Thanks for meeting with me for this 1-2-1. This is your time to share feedback, present issues, and improve.

Drew: Okay. That's new.

Mia: So, when you thought about meeting with me, what went through your mind?

Drew: I thought about the issues I'm having with scheduling my team.

Mia: Would you like to focus on those issues? Or is there something else on your mind?

Drew: Sure. Solving the scheduling issue would make my life easier.

Mia: Great. If you were to look back at the end of our conversation and felt it was successful, what would that look like?

Drew (Pause): I guess I'd figure out how to find an effective way for my team to meet our deadlines because it matters to all of our internal partners. We sometimes fall behind. Then we start blaming each other.

Mia: Well, let's start there. You'd like to be coached on how to help your team meet deadlines. You are very concerned about the impact it has on the team and others with whom you coordinate.

Drew: Yeah, I think that's it.

Ascertain

In his famous TED talk, Simon Sinek told millions of people how important the *why* of what we do is to business. He said, "Very few people or companies can clearly articulate WHY they do rather than WHAT they do. By WHY, I mean your purpose, cause, or belief." Simon's point was that articulating a compelling reason and meaning for what we do fuels alignment and gives vision to where we are going.

Imagine you've started on your journey. Your head isn't down because you're ascertaining your surroundings and what you see down the road—and all the factors that affect your next steps. Ascertaining sharpens your vision.

In the *Ascertain* stage of coaching, you help the person discover what led them to coaching, clarify their goals, and understand what makes it important to them. This stage of the PASN model is focused on awareness and exploration. What led to the current situation, and what's motivating them to change? What do they value, and what's important to them? In the previous example, Mia might explore whether this team ever met their deadlines and, if so, what was different about them or the situation in those cases.

People respond to *Purpose* questions with a wide range of responses, all of which require clarification in the *Ascertain* stage. For example: "I want to make a decision about this person's value to the team." Or "I need to decide the best strategy for my project." Then, the person being coached and the leader who's coaching them learn how he or she perceives the situation and what actions, beliefs, and emotions are involved. "I feel badly that I convinced this person to leave another team and join ours, and now she isn't performing well." Or "I'm concerned that our suppliers are shifting, and prices will be over the top for us. I don't want to fail." The coach helps the person uncover motivations, perceptions, and needs because they indicate road signs *and* obstacles to achieving their purpose.

On the roadmap, *Ascertain* is about discovery. What is my reality, and how does the situation look to others? Often the longest stage of the journey, this stage explores in detail his or her perspective and data, including personal knowledge like strengths, mistakes, fears, and joys. As he or she is being coached, they're also discovering how they see others and how they believe others see the situation. They're becoming aware of their assumptions and what may not be clear to them. Coaching encourages others to have a 360-degree view of what's going on inside and out. As you can imagine, listening actively, empathizing, and understanding are keys at this stage.

Margo was wondering why her team leader, Katie, was avoiding a conversation with one of her team members about their performance. In the Ascertain stage, she helped Katie identify what was holding her back.

Margo: *Tell me more about how you usually respond to performance issues.*

Katie: *Well, it's not usually a problem. I make sure we both understand expectations, and then we figure out how the person will improve things.*

Margo: *Sounds like you're comfortable having a candid conversation and making a plan. What makes David different?*

Katie (thinking for a moment): *First of all, he just had his fourth child. I'm concerned about what might happen if this role doesn't work out. Also, he was transferred to me, and I'm not sure about what he does.*

Margo: *I appreciate how you care about your team, Katie. It sounds like you have two issues: you aren't clear about his role, and you're concerned about the impact on David if he doesn't succeed. Anything else?*

Katie: *I want my whole team to succeed. In my first meetings with others on the team, they shared that David's performance is creating problems for them.*

Margo: *You began our conversation with how you usually address performance issues. What's missing in this situation?*

Katie: *Well first, I don't know much about his role or the expectations that were set up before I came. Second, I don't have his trust. We're just getting to know each other. Finally, I don't have enough information about where we're going as a team or how everyone's role fits in. It's new to all of us.*

Margo: *Because this is a new role for you, there's a lot you don't know. You haven't settled on where the team's going, everyone's role, and, in particular, you're just beginning to build trust with David. You're concerned about the team's feedback about David but don't feel comfortable approaching him right now. What would make you less hesitant about approaching David?*

Katie: *I think that's absolutely true. I felt pressure to follow up on the team members' complaints right away. But now that I think*

> *about it, I need to dig in and understand David and his role*
> *before I decide to act on that feedback. In addition, it's my role*
> *to provide clarity for the team. I would be less hesitant if I were*
> *clear about everyone's role.*

Margo: *I just heard the words clarity, clear, and understand. What's*
becoming clearer to you?

Katie: *I need to step back and assess everyone's role and contribution,*
including David's. I guess I was so concerned that he would fail
and the ramifications for his family that I didn't think through
my role and contribution.

Because leaders are often such good problem solvers, they tend to shortchange the crucial *Ascertain* stage and move right to solving the problem. They assume they know what the problem is and don't bother to explore what else might be going on. As a result, they might not focus on the bigger picture or find the core issue. Through Mia's coaching, Katie learned that the core issue was more about her lack of clarity as a leader than about David or the feedback she was hearing about him. She realized that until she worked with the team to figure out team roles and direction, feedback would be premature. When leaders don't spend time helping the person to ascertain what's involved, they take a shortcut through the woods only to find they're at the end of a cliff. Shortcuts, usually punctuated by superficial questions, often end up with solutions without substance.

Here's an example of how what I call "problem-solving pseudo-coaching" can look in a situation where the person being coached is concerned about a new team member's ability to succeed.

"What do you want your team to look like? How is Anne not fitting in? What are your options to move her off your team?"

We call this *machine gun questioning*. You want to drill the person and solve the problem quickly. However, you haven't explored how the person came to the issue or, most importantly, their vision of what it would look like when the problem's solved. In contrast, coaching helps him or her identify the path they want to trek and the destination that's most meaningful to them. Here's an example of what that kind of coaching can look like:

"It sounds like you're concerned about Anne fitting in. Tell me about that." Or "It sounds like you feel responsible for Anne's success because you pushed for her to be on your team. How did you push her?"

The *Ascertain* stage of the coaching journey makes few assumptions. Keep your conclusions to yourself—they belong to you, not the other person. Through listening, encouraging, and asking great questions, you're increasing awareness and bringing clarity. Awareness of their motivations, values, surroundings, and clarity about where they want to go. You're helping them see and feel what was previously invisible to them.

When you *Ascertain*, you may end up returning to the first step to redefine the issue or problem in a different way. "You're clear that Anne is not performing well in spite of your coaching. You feel guilty that you made a bad decision and haven't set her up for success. Is there anything else that's going on that's making you feel stumped?"

Coaching questions during this stage are very open. Areas of exploration include motivation, core values, pressure, stress, and emotions.

- How important is that to you?
- What's the impact on you and others? Impact on the business?
- What exactly makes this challenging for you?
- What does that (success, fear, etc.) look like and feel like?
- Can you share an example of what you mean?
- What's your contribution to this situation?
- How do others see this situation?
- What are the long-term implications if this situation doesn't change?

These questions and the deep listening that usually follows help the person become more clear about what they want and need and what they can change to get there. The movement forward springs out of this discovery. We see what wasn't there, and the best path begins to emerge.

Strategizing—Which Path Forward is the Best?

The journey continues, and coaching has helped the person you're coaching assess themselves and the situation. Clarifying the heart of the issue in the *Ascertain* stage of the roadmap often lifts the fog, and—*voila!*—possibilities emerge. I've often been surprised about how asking questions not only generates insight but also clear actions for resolving an issue. If you ask, "What choices are emerging from our conversations that might address the issue we defined at the beginning?" it can help the person gain insight. Seeing the path forward can lift the fog and uncover possibilities.

It's okay to focus on a single leg of the path rather than planning out an entire journey. Strategizing often means exploring solutions in terms of *what else?* When the person being coached sees the full array of possible paths forward, the best solution emerges. It may feel right emotionally, and that feeling may result from prioritizing what's most important. Strategizing frees us to consider choices and decide.

"I know now that Anne's role doesn't use her strengths and that I don't have a position for her that does. I feel strongly, however, that she has strengths that can be used somewhere in this company. I also see that she isn't happy and probably doesn't feel successful. I can continue to ignore everything, and my team will continue to be frustrated. Or I can talk with her about what she's experiencing and try to determine the resources that will help both of us make changes."

In the *Strategy* stage, keep focusing on the desired outcome and generate several ways to achieve what's wanted. Often, the person lands on what—to them—will help them move forward. Then you can explore the pluses and the minuses of each. Asking questions like these can help the person weigh their options:

- If you were successful, what would that look like?

- What's possible here? What else is possible? What else?
- Which option do you feel best about and why?
- When have you been in this situation before, and what have you done?

When you ask strategy questions, you must also actively listen carefully, so the person you're coaching can hear their wisdom.

NEXT—The Final Stage of the PASN Model

If your conversation doesn't result in the person moving toward a goal, preferred state, or an action, then it isn't coaching. It's just a good conversation about an issue. The final part of PASN is to give the person an opportunity to articulate what the coaching session meant to them, what they gained, and what they're committed to doing.

In the next stage, the coaching escalates toward action. What comes *NEXT*? Choosing an action builds on the motivation and clarity you've set up in the three previous stages. When you arrive at *NEXT*, you help him or her create a specific plan for the next step to reach their goal.

I've learned that my idea of what's next or best isn't necessarily what's right for someone else. Often, the people I coach come up with options or a plan I'd never imagined—or one that I doubted would work. Yet, most of the time, it did. Their solutions came from understanding what *they* wanted, who *they* were, and the resources *they* could use. The coaching process respects that the person, not the coach, determines their future.

Coach for Action Steps. The coach's role at this step is to help the person articulate specific action steps. Vague self-promises like, "I will talk to them" or "I'll find time to communicate more" won't usually result in the changes they want. At this point, the leader/coach leads them toward a tangible plan by asking questions like:

- When do you plan on starting or doing the next step?

- What, specifically, will that conversation include?
- How will you know it's been successful?

The *NEXT* phase can also inspire creativity. I never forgot the intriguing plan that Kevin, a leader who'd received interesting feedback from his team, developed. Although he was a good listener, he didn't spontaneously share enough of his thoughts with them. To the team, their interactions felt one-sided. After exploring their feedback, Kevin was ready to devise a plan for changing how he interacted with his team. Kevin's strategy was to put ten coins in his pocket every day. Every time he spoke to someone personally, which included sharing something about himself, he would transfer one coin to his other pocket. His goal was ten transferred coins a day—or ten interactions. That way, he was both reminded of his goal *and* kept track of his success. It wasn't long until his new behavior yielded immediate appreciation. It worked beautifully for him.

Strategies can be very simple, like "reach out to this person to ask for help on my project." Keep in mind that coaching only works if effective strategies are identified by the person being coached, not you. Their vision, choice, and motivation are the keys to their success.

Anticipating Obstacles. Once a path is chosen, you can help the person to identify potential obstacles. Obstacles are often hidden and can represent resistance to change, even when you or your team wants to change. When you help others identify potential roadblocks to their plan, they are better able to clear the path forward. The obstacles may be internal (fear of failing) or external (others won't respond positively). Identifying obstacles helps prepare the person for challenges to their action plan. Taking time to explore the question, "What might get in your way?" can help illuminate unanticipated consequences and engage their brain to prepare to overcome them. Identifying potential barriers may also propel you both back into the *Ascertain* and *Strategy* stages to clear the path. Identifying obstacles have their own set of coaching questions:

- How will you get in your way?
- What are the internal and external barriers?
- What may stop you or slow you down?

NEXT also means that you help the person decide how they'll execute their chosen plan. It might be as specific as identifying who, what, where, and when. Throughout the *NEXT* stage, they choose and, as a result, they become clear and committed. *NEXT* makes it more likely that your coaching will result in an outcome that is measurable and to which the person is accountable—to themselves. You will support their plan, but the path forward is their choice. As at the beginning of the PASN Roadmap, you're challenging them to reflect and focus. *NEXT* provides the step that brings all the coaching together and makes it actionable.

Coach The Person, Not the Problem

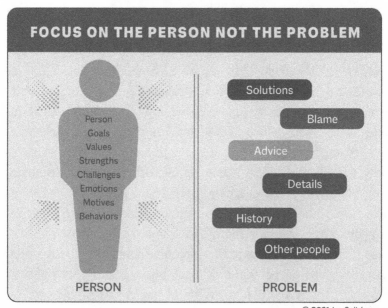

© 2021 Jan Salisbury

I hope you've noticed that every coaching example in this book is primarily focused on the person or team, not the issue or other people. Focusing on people is the standard for professional coaches and leaders who coach. We reflect back the person's perspectives and emotions. We encourage them to use their strengths and take a step forward. Our coaching questions help unlock their motivations, desires, and goals. In that process, the person also explores the focus of their goals and feelings, e.g., the issue or challenge. And in the end, only that person can take the action they've chosen. As Marcia Reynolds, Master Certified Executive Coach, says in her book *Coach the Person, Not the Problem,* "Coaching is valuable because none of us transform our thinking on our own." Furthermore, she says, "Coaching is an effective technology for helping people quickly reframe, shift perspective and redefine themselves and their situations."[23] When we focus solely on the problem, issue, or goal, it becomes about our perceptions or about others, not about the person who will choose how to act. Telling someone to own our stories and ideas doesn't empower them to think and grow. It's only a transfer of information.

While it's tempting to follow your curiosity about an issue or problem, succumbing to your interest in a topic will ultimately undermine the effectiveness of your coaching. Questions such as, "Wow, when did so-and-so first have that problem? What was their background? What does HR think about this problem?" aren't effective in coaching. More importantly, it won't develop the person you're coaching or motivate them to change their thinking or behavior. That's the inside job that coaching does so well.

When leaders use the PASN Roadmap, they're not telling their employees what to do. The roadmap and skills help those they coach to discover the insights and skills and resources they need to accomplish a task or reach their goals. The leader/coach owns the process of coaching, and the person being coached owns their story and the outcome. That's the partnership of coaching.

Using The Roadmap—A Few Things to Remember: *The Road Isn't Always Straight.*

While the coaching roadmap can help the person you're coaching resolve an issue, it isn't always a straight path. There may be detours because there are relevant areas to explore. That exploration may lead to a core issue or one that is a lynchpin in the situation. And there's no direct route to truth and awareness. Sometimes the path meanders, and then suddenly, you're viewing a magnificent valley. Eureka! Change tends to happen in small steps. Sometimes you may have to revisit an issue a few times.

Stay on the PASN Roadmap

Always keep the roadmap in your brain or in front of you. Take your time, especially in the *Ascertain* stage, but move on in the time you've allotted. The roadmap is the key to helping the person find a solution or plan. Slowly get to know the purpose of each stage and the questions that may be most appropriate. As professional coaches, we prepare questions before we meet with our clients. As a leader who coaches, you can also prepare a set of questions for each stage. While you may not use the exact questions in your conversation, preparing them in advance helps to create a coaching mindset for asking, not telling.

Use All the Coaching Skills in Each Stage

Finally, don't become so focused on the questions that you forget that active listening and encouragement help the person discover the issues and their choices for themselves. Each of the skills reinforces a different aspect of each coaching step.

Use the Roadmap to Empower and Develop

It's easy to see the PASN roadmap as a problem-solving checklist. It isn't. Coaching intentionally and using a flexible roadmap will slow down decision making in the person you're coaching, so they can address the right issue and look for the best answer.

Finally, as a leader who coaches, decide when coaching is appropriate for the situation. If someone isn't ready to be coached or isn't open to owning where they're going or solving the problem, use another one of your coaching hats. If you don't yet have sufficient trust with the person, save the coaching hat until a time when you do. Or if you're responsible for making a decision, don't use coaching to distract. For example, coaching isn't a substitute for the responsibility you have to determine if the right people are on the bus or if a person's behavior and values prevent them from fitting on your bus.

The PASN model is a guideline for your coaching success. Give yourself time to practice and learn it. Coaching is also filled with humor and light moments. My coaching conversations are often mixed with laughter. We crack up at ourselves and situations, which allows us to share great moments of connection and to detach from ourselves.

NEXT

1. Buy a notebook to keep track of your coaching. Write down the PASN model in a way that makes sense to you. Keep questions and notes about coachable moments. Then find a few minutes a week to review and reflect.
2. Choose a specific meeting or person with whom to practice the PASN roadmap. It might be a friend or colleague. Identify a few questions for each stage. (See Appendix B for ideas). Commit to making it through all four steps.
3. Reflect on what went well. How did the other person react? What will you do differently next time?
4. Reflect on what you learned about coaching after you practice.

9

BEING COACHED: ONE STORY

"When there is trust, conflict becomes nothing but the pursuit of truth, an attempt to find the best possible answer."

—Patrick Lencioni

THE COACH APPROACH is an interdependent dynamic between the coaching mindset, presence, and coaching skills. We refer to this coaching model as the PASN Roadmap:[24]

- **Purpose:** Define your purpose as a leader.
- **Ascertain:** Take a coaching skills self-audit.
- **Strategize the Way:** Generate multiple solutions and possible actions.
- **Next:** Identify obstacles and create action steps.

These coaching behaviors and beliefs show up in unison to empower and develop those around you. I've included examples of coaching taken from the stories leaders have shared with me over the years. In addition to practicing coaching, the best leaders who coach employ a coach of their own, so they can grow themselves and experience coaching from the perspective of being coached. Being coached really makes coaching come alive and provides valuable insight into how and why coaching works. Before we move on to other ways you can lead by coaching, let's consider the perspective of a leader being coached by *her* leader.

> *Amy, a marketing director, was preparing for her 1-2-1 with Justin, the owner and CEO of SOFTMAX, a high-tech business. She knew she had to choose an area of focus, but the one she felt most concerned about felt too risky to process with her boss. She didn't want to be judged for being wrong. In a nutshell, Amy was disappointed that Max, her peer and sales manager, wasn't following through with their agreed-upon plan. She also knew that Justin liked Max. She wondered if Justin would be impartial enough to help her. She decided to approach the topic indirectly and see if she got some help that way.*
>
> *When Amy entered Justin's office, she noticed the stunning photographs of mountains, lakes, and rivers on his walls. Everyone knew that Justin loved being in the mountains, and she shared his affinity for the outdoors. Justin was seated at a round table and welcomed her. He began by asking how she was doing and what she and her team were celebrating. Amy was excited about her team's progress and happy to share. Her team of three was completing projects on time, and they were jazzed about the results they were starting to see in terms of online customers. Then Justin asked the question she knew was coming: "What's up with you today, Amy, and what would you like to focus on?"*
>
> *Amy took a breath and said, "Well, we do fine when it's our project, but when we're working with sales, we don't seem to be aligned on the plan. I'm wondering what we could do differently."*
>
> *Justin asked several questions and finally restated the key issue. "Amy, it sounds like you want to figure out how to get your team and*

the sales team on the same page, so you can implement the plan you and Max have made."

Amy felt both queasy and relieved. She thought for a moment. "Yeah, I think you nailed it. Somehow the follow-up from our agreements isn't working at all."

Justin reflected back to Amy the anger he thought he heard. "You sound angry with Max . . ."

Amy reframed it. "Maybe disappointed is a better word." She sighed and thought, There, the cat is out of the bag.

Justin was silent. Then he asked her, "Was there a time when you two and the two teams were working well? If so, what happened? If not, what would it look like if things were working well?"

Amy realized that she'd never thought about that question. She looked out the window and tried to remember a time when it did work. "About a year ago, we were working well together," she said. Then she described what happened last year. "Max and I had multiple meetings. We really focused on being clear about the expectations for the project and how our teams could communicate. Then we had a meeting with both of our teams. It went well."

Although Amy was uncomfortable with Justin delving into her real feelings, she also felt relieved to say how she felt out loud, and she began to see the situation differently.

Justin reflected what she said and then went to a different place. "What's been getting in the way of repeating what worked before?"

Again, Amy felt uncomfortable. "I'm not sure. Max and I kind of assumed that our teams would work it out. They never did. My team isn't happy about it. They don't feel successful."

Justin nodded, and Amy felt better. He's not judging me, *she thought. Then he said, "Sounds like neither you nor your team is feeling positive about how you're working with sales on this project. Tell me more about what you're thinking and feeling."*

Amy didn't hesitate. "I feel pissed that Max isn't leading his team."

Justin followed up with, "What have you done with that feeling?"

"Nothing," Amy said. "I just hoped it would be better next time we had a deadline. But it wasn't."

Justin nodded. "So, you hoped it would change and didn't act on your experience. Did anything hold you back, Amy?"

Yeah, Amy thought to herself, Max's ego. But she simply said, "I didn't want to create more conflict."

"Anything else?" Justin asked. Although Amy knew it probably wouldn't cut it with Justin, she just sat in silence.

She was grateful when Justin brought the conversations back to her goal: aligning both the sales and marketing teams to execute their plan effectively. "Is that what you still want? Any ideas on how to move forward?"

"Yes!" she exclaimed. "I guess we need to start checking in and communicating about expectations and not make assumptions."

Justin circled back to what might be holding Amy back. "What exactly are you concerned about that would get in the way of starting to meet and communicate?"

Amy realized she needed to talk about what was hard for her if she was going to solve the problem. "Okay, to be honest, my relationship with Max isn't in a good place. It makes sense that if I want our teams to work better, Max and I need to improve our communication."

Justin nodded again and said, "It's tough to have a key peer relationship working poorly. One strength I see with you, Amy, is your candor and how much you care about healthy relationships in our company." Amy nodded.

Justin realized that their scheduled time together was ending. "Amy, since we only have a few minutes left in our 1-2-1, I'm wondering what's become clear for you as a next step. Also, I understand there are many aspects of this situation we haven't clarified in this meeting, and I'm willing to meet again if you'd like."

Amy had refocused her efforts, not on changing Max but on what was possible for her. "I think I'm ready to initiate conversations with Max and explore our perspectives. I'm going to suggest that we go back to how we worked together last year. Then I'll ask for his suggestions. That's my first step. Second, I want to define what I need from Max to work better with him—communication on things like email, meetings, etc. Of course, I'll invite him to tell me his needs as well. If the situation still hasn't changed, I'll make a time to meet with you before our next scheduled 1-2-1."

"How do you feel about that plan, Amy, and when will you plan to meet with Max?" Justin asked.

"It's a good beginning," replied Amy. "Actually, I'll initiate a meeting in the next couple of days and meet before the end of the week. It helps to have a direction and plan to solve the situation. Thank you."

The coaching dialogue between Justin and Amy is only part of the conversation that realistically would take place. To address Amy's presented issue, there would need to be many more reflections and questions to facilitate the PASN Roadmap. Justin's role in this conversation was simply to coach Amy, not to jump in to address other issues or offer his solutions. Yet I hope you can see how Justin's coaching skills led to a willingness on Amy's part to implement a specific plan she generated. That's the self-accountability coaching generates. I can't underestimate the importance of empowering others to come up with a plan about what they want to do next. We spotlight this in the next chapter.

NEXT

- Review the example above and identify the skills and steps in the PASN Roadmap Justin used.
- Imagine a past or future conversation that you could coach. Write out potential questions, statements of encouragement, and the PASN Roadmap.

10

COACH WHAT'S STRONG, NOT WHAT'S WRONG

"When well-being comes from engaging our strengths and virtues, our lives are imbued with authenticity."

—Martin Seligman

MARTIN SELIGMAN'S QUOTE recognizes that to lead a fulfilling life and address challenges successfully, we must be aware of what's strong in us. Seligman, the former president of the American Psychological Association, founded the positive psychology movement and urged psychologists to study the virtues and strengths of people in order to balance the focus on problems and dysfunction.[25] In other words, if we're resilient and know what we love to do, our intrinsic motivation is more likely to lead to high engagement and performance. In coaching, being able to balance the focus on problems or deficits with strengths and knowing how to use them is essential.

Intuitively, leaders understand the importance of knowing one's strengths. For example, good leaders hire team members who have strengths different than their own because they recognize that diverse strengths create great results. Knowing one's strengths also spotlights areas of challenge. Many entrepreneurs with whom I've worked realize that their strength of envisioning a future or product and representing their company's brand to customers is thwarted when they're mired in the day-to-day minutiae. Not only do they not enjoy the details, but focusing on the details keeps them from the very tasks they relish and are necessary to grow the business. Leaders who are self-aware eventually hire others team members who excel at those tasks and roles. They are, as they say, in their element. Finally, when we're in environments and roles that value and use our strengths, we're more willing to take risks and play where no one else is playing.

How Coaching Defines Strength

Our definition of strength in coaching and organizational development is different than the one commonly used. You may do many things well, but you don't necessarily enjoy engaging that part of you. Rather than just focusing on what a person does well, we define *strength* as a "pre-existing capacity for a way of behaving, thinking, or feeling that is authentic and energizing to the user and enables optimal functioning."[26] *Preexisting* might refer to a combination of natural tendencies, cultural influences, and learning experiences. There also may be strengths that are yet to be discovered.

What parts of our role do we really enjoy? What energizes our ability to perform? Janelle, a leader with whom I worked, lamented that she didn't like planning the details of her vision. However, she loved collaborating and relationships. Identifying her strengths helped her to get unstuck from avoiding a strategic planning process. She now asked herself, *How can I engage my staff to help me create the details of my strategic plan?* She had plenty of people on her team who excelled at details, and she dove into engaging them by using her strength in collaboration.

Strengths evolve, and over time, they can change. Some things we enjoyed and received pleasure from doing years ago no longer appeal to us. We develop new strengths throughout our careers and discover that we perform best when we're deploying them.

These strengths include a wide variety of behaviors and characteristics:

- Special knowledge or skills
- Written communication that's clear and personable
- Listening and communicating with others
- Project management—organizing a project and deploying a team to accomplish the mission
- Presenting and enrolling others in a vision or plan
- Connecting and building customer relationships
- Hiring and building cohesive teams
- Expressing empathy or caring

When I'm coaching, I share the coaching definition of strengths to open the door for others to see and feel their strengths. I want them to tap into what excites them, what motivates them, and what they're doing when they're their best selves. It's not simply what others think they do well, although that can be helpful to explore. When you coach, you're inviting others to own what's intrinsically effective and motivating.

Imagine the productivity and happiness index leaders could achieve if everyone were allowed to fully utilize their strengths in their roles! While it's true that all roles involve unpleasant or depleting tasks, research clearly shows that if someone is spending too much of their time engaged in these activities, their performance will not be exemplary, and they're more likely to leave the position. During the Great Resignation of the pandemic, we saw many people leave their jobs because they were no longer using the best of themselves.

Strength Spotting

How can you help others spot their strengths? Can assessments help? How can you help a person own their strengths and leverage them when they're making important decisions or addressing challenges? Finally, how can you integrate strength awareness into your organizational culture?

Unfortunately, if you just ask people what their strengths are, they're likely to give you the first definition—what they do well. If you ask them what they love to do in their role and what gives them energy and joy, you're likely to receive a very different answer. In addition, many of us are taught not to toot our own horns. We believe that means not acknowledging what we've done well and instead pointing out all the ways we could be better. As a result, as a culture, we tend to undervalue our strengths and overvalue our challenges or deficits. As human beings, we must have both to grow. Here are a few ideas to help others discover their strengths (and help you discover yours too).

Peak Performance

In my first coaching sessions, I almost always ask my clients to describe a situation in which they performed exceptionally well and enjoyed doing so—a time when they were at their peak. What were the circumstances, what did they do, how did they interact, etc.? Then I ask them how others might've identified their strengths in that situation. Would they agree? Of all the ways in which they performed and behaved, what gave them the most energy?

One woman who organized a very successful national conference told me that she loved being the visionary, developing the dedicated team, and bringing great speakers together to accomplish the vision. The details of payment, sponsorship, and constant communication were draining, and for that reason, she said she wouldn't do it again.

However, she saw clearly that inspiring others with her vision, bringing together diverse skills to accomplish the task, and enticing great speakers to present was motivating, and she was proud of the results. She also realized that when she lost sight of doing that meaningful work or didn't seek out others with whom to collaborate, she wasn't at her best. She used that knowledge to make good choices about how she could contribute to projects successfully.

Using your coaching to encourage and listen actively helps draw out people's experience when they share their peak performance. Watch them nod and light up when they acknowledge the truth about their strengths.

A Time You Were Resilient

Another source of identifying strengths is looking at the way people respond to challenges. When you coach someone who's struggling with a difficult situation, ask them about other challenging situations in which they were effective. What did they learn about themselves, and how did they overcome the situation? What worked? When you help them name the *what* in a way that showcases their strengths, they can better consider how to apply those strengths to their current challenge.

In the previous example I gave, the leader recognized the joy she received from creatively addressing a community need. "What would you call that strength of yours?" I asked.

She paused and shared, "I guess it's two things—being able to think out of the box and my passion to improve my community."

"Are there any opportunities to use those strengths in this situation?" I asked.

She began to challenge herself to think creatively. She lit up. Possibilities poured forth. She knew she could implement one in particular, and she was willing to give it a try.

Observing Strengths Firsthand

As a leader who coaches, you have the opportunity to hear and see strengths firsthand, and this gives you an advantage over professional coaches. As a result, you can share directly how someone's strengths are being expressed. For example, when others are sharing their stories, notice the positive nonverbal expression when they describe what they did. Notice how much pleasure they appear to receive from accomplishing an activity.

> *Derek was learning to be a CEO. In a family-owned business, he was the youngest to ascend to the position, and he was both excited about learning and apprehensive about whether he would succeed. When he started talking about the individual store managers and how much he enjoyed helping them succeed, he brightened and smiled. When asked if developing his team was a strength and joy, he nodded vigorously. "I do love it; I could also be better at doing it!" He didn't enjoy setting expectations and accountability, but he realized that his ability to establish relationships and encourage others would pave the way for conversations involving expectations and feedback. He was ready to build on his strength to communicate clear expectations.*

Identifying strengths doesn't mean there aren't any areas for improvement. Understanding our strengths also builds confidence to tackle new challenges.

Strength Assessments

As I pointed out in the first chapter, the deficit model of focusing primarily on our weaknesses rarely works. As Martin Seligman says, "Focus on what is strong, not what is wrong."[27] It can be disheartening when we spend too much time defining ourselves by what we can't or don't do well. It can also become a self-fulfilling prophecy. By minimizing what we do well and what fills us up, we're missing a core ingredient of our future success. In addition, we have deep histories affected by our gender, family, and culture that can undermine our understanding of how important our strengths are. The title of this book highlights that coaching unleashes the geniuses, or strengths, of those around us. When that happens, they can tap into deep reservoirs of resources and energy.

In addition to exploring individually what a person loves to do—and does well—you can use standardized assessments to unlock the strength door. Most valid assessments require an outside expert or consultant to administer the assessment and interpret the results for an individual or a team. There are some assessments, however, that you can self-administer. For example, Patrick Lencioni's "The 6 Types of Working Genius," helps teams and individuals understand what areas of work are draining and what brings them joy. Scored and interpreted by The Table Group, the assessment offers great face validity without judgment.[28] Additionally, the Gallup Strength Finder can be taken by buying the book *Now, Discover Your Strengths* and using the code provided.[29] You receive a report of statistically defined strengths that Gallup has identified and discusses in the book. Another self-administered choice you and your team can use is the VIA Survey of Character Strengths created by Martin Seligman and a large team of psychologists.[30] They spent ten years gathering data about universally defined psychological ingredients for displaying virtues or human goodness.

For example, IBM Australia had measurable results that fostered employee engagement using VIA Signature Character Strengths.[31] They discovered that once people knew their character strengths, they were able to set stretching goals for their performance. Also, when leaders shared their profiles, they deepened their understanding of one another and what was most gratifying and important for them in the workplace.

Regardless of what assessment you or the person you're coaching use, remember these guidelines:

- Many assessments are best used and shared in a team situation as a way of capitalizing on team strengths. This increases trust in the team and deemphasizes the vulnerability of the individual. If you're giving the assessment to a group for general development, always consider inviting an expert to create the context and interpretation of the results. If not, have everyone read the preliminary material or book to understand what the assessment measures are and how the definitions are defined.

- Only use an assessment if it can help with the goals of the coaching and the person is ready and wants to receive the information. Information about oneself, even if it's positive, can be challenging.

- The person who takes the assessment ultimately decides whether and how strong the strength identified is true for them. No assessment is infallible, and if the person doesn't accept the results, it's a non-starter. Go with what they see and accept.

- All assessments, even valid ones, are slices of who we are. They never represent all our capabilities, styles, etc. Again, provide this context about strengths and communicate that, in the end, people know themselves better than the assessments do.

- First, take the assessment yourself. If you have a coach, ask them to help you use it to learn about yourself. You can then share examples of your strengths and anything else you've discovered.

Leveraging Strengths

Elevating awareness of one's strengths is a fundamental tool in coaching. Naming and understanding the strength is, by itself, motivating and supportive. While our strengths may be momentarily hidden to us, being reminded of the value we bring and the delight we experience in certain situations and behaviors is uplifting. Furthermore, our successes and strengths are valuable tools when we're confronted with challenges or are seeking to improve. Here are some additional examples of leveraging strengths:

In her 1-2-1 with her leader, Brandon, Kim was struggling with how to break her habit of quickly sharing her honest opinion when a challenging issue was on the table. She identified one of her strengths as collaborating and working on a team.

"How does that strength show up for you?" asked Brandon.

Kim pondered for a moment. "Well, usually I listen and ask others what they think works best."

"What about listening and being curious about how others' perspectives work?"

Kim took her time to think about his question. "I think everyone, including me, appreciates it when others listen and care enough to ask for their opinion."

"I'm wondering," continued Brandon, "how that strength could help you with your feedback."

Kim responded quickly. "Instead of putting my opinions out there, I could listen first and then ask questions. I'll still share honestly, but I can see how putting the team first would be helpful for all of us." She saw the connection and created a plan for bringing that strength to meetings.

Jason told his peer Sula, "I don't know about you, but I'm working long hours, and the results I'm achieving don't feel like enough. I'm exhausted and uninspired."

Sula looked up from the table where they were sitting and drinking coffee. "Well," she asked, "how much time do you spend doing the things you really love?"

"None," he replied. "I love to work as a team, and this is all solo work. It's dispiriting, and my department's behind."

"So there's absolutely no room to work with others on these projects?" Sula responded, looking doubtful.

"Hey Sula, you're right. I've been so used to working from home during COVID-19, I haven't thought about ways I can reach out. I'm going to adjust my schedule and prioritize calling others to get their input and perspective on my project. Just saying that feels better."

"Great idea, Jason. It's been hard for me to adjust to working from home and now coming in to work too. I've always enjoyed working with you on a project—let me know how it goes."

Organizations can also adopt a strength-based approach to their culture and development. The Northern Technology Council worked to support technology companies throughout the state. Here's their story:

We had a toxic environment for a long time. People were told what to do and then criticized when they didn't do it just right. We weren't a team—instead, everyone was loyal to their departments without a sense of support for one another. People were leaving.

Our new CEO made sure culture was a priority. We worked hard to identify key values and communicate openly with one another. Then we decided to become a strength-based culture, first using the Gallop Strength Finder. Every team member learned not only about their own strengths and how they could use those to be more engaged but also about the strengths of others. We came to appreciate the way diverse strengths made a stronger team and how we could value one another's strengths. We hired coaches and consultants to help us understand and leverage everyone's strengths. Bringing the strength-based mindset to our meetings and our 1-2-1s became a habit.

Soon, a more positive culture began to emerge. We learned how to communicate without fear and communicate about conflict. The leadership team realized that empowerment was an important part of our new culture. The Leaders Who Coach: Essentials *program was an opportunity for us to learn the coach approach to build collaboration and develop our teams. We rotated leaders through the program (including our CEO) and met regularly just to focus on learning from one another about coaching, using triads, and discussions about challenges and successes. We also realized that Strength Finder was just one way to identify strengths, so we integrated a program called* Cloverleaf *that allows us to use multiple assessments to help us become aware of our styles and strengths. Our culture now collaborates, communicates better regarding conflict, and sees all interactions as opportunities for growth. Coaching has become a valued skill set that all our leaders use for collaborating and building the organization.*

Overusing Strengths—Mindful Strength Deployment

I believe that awareness of self is key for optimal performance. Unfortunately, we're often running so fast to accomplish and perform that we don't stop to reflect. When was the last time you received 360-degree feedback that was meant to develop you as opposed to evaluate you?

Coaching accelerates awareness, revealing what we do and don't know or understand about ourselves. It's particularly challenging to see how a strength that feels natural and successful much of the time can be overused and can undermine our effectiveness. The Center for Creative Leadership, founded in 1970, develops leaders both through coaching and by teaching leaders to coach. As they studied derailed executives, they found that the least effective managers overrated their effectiveness, and the most effective managers underrated their effectiveness. In other words, even effective leaders were not aware of strengths they could be using. They also found that 40 percent or more of promoted leaders weren't successful—their organizations never provided the development to help leaders identify strengths that would or wouldn't work in their new positions.[32]

The impact of COVID-19 on leadership development has yet to be studied. However, we do know that many hybrid workplaces aren't investing enough in developing new leaders who are stepping up quickly as other leaders retire or are leaving the workplace. The capacity of leaders to coach others is a powerful strategy to fill this gap.

One leader with whom I worked was a nationally recognized consultant who became a member of a high-level leadership team of a company. Jack's knowledge and ability to influence others to adopt strategies and implement technology were renowned. However, early in his tenure, he received strong feedback that his communication with peers was off-putting, even overbearing. He always came across as the expert. That wasn't Jack's intention—he was just using a well-honed strength from his role as a consultant. He hadn't adapted to his new role, which required leading inside the organization. How else could he participate in the peer leadership meetings?

In our coaching, Jack recognized that part of his success as a consultant was his ability to listen deeply to the concerns and perspectives of others. Peers, he reasoned, turned off when he came across as the person with the answers. So, he mindfully switched to his listening strengths. The results were immediate. When Jack listened first and shared his perspective sparingly, others opened up and began to connect and value him more.

As a leader who coaches, it's essential to help others dial into the places where their strengths work best and with whom. Mindfully deploying one's strengths is another step in developing self-awareness and becoming more effective.

Coaching develops others through a combination of support, challenge, and focus. Employing strengths fills up our reservoir of motivation and joy. When we can access skills and capabilities that have been not only successful but also provide inner satisfaction, coaching works to develop the whole person or team. When you coach others, help them use their strengths when they're tackling challenges. Then your coaching will help build their confidence to take risks and persevere.

NEXT

- Using the exercises in this chapter, identify the strengths you have. Check with others who know you well. What do they see?
- Take an easily accessible valid assessment that spotlights your values, style, or needs. Share what you learn with others.
- Make a list of direct reports, peers, or team members. Identify two strengths you see in them.
- Begin asking strength questions in your conversations with others or with your team (see Appendix A).
- When you're having a coaching conversation with someone, notice what strength they're showing. Share that with them.

11

WHO OWNS ACCOUNTABILITY IN COACHING?

"We don't develop people. We equip others to develop themselves."

—David Peterson

EXECUTIVE COACH DAVID Peterson's quote is the essence of why coaching is so powerful. Coaching inspires others to reflect, decide, and move forward.

You likely became a leader because of your unwavering commitment not just to getting things done, but to making sure everyone is doing the right thing. As a leader, you're responsible for results—meeting goals, developing a culture that fosters engagement and collaboration, and achieving the mission of the organization. However, *everyone* on your team is also accountable for working toward these results. When we coach, we automatically shift ownership for solutions and follow-through from ourselves to the person being coached. It's a shift that most leaders desperately want but don't understand how to do. In this chapter, we describe how coaching facilitates that shift.

Remember, when you coach, you let go of *your* notions of what should be done and how. The coaching process we describe builds on accountability every step of the way.

Accountability Every Step of the Way

Remember the first step in the coaching process? You begin your coaching by discovering the person's purpose and the outcome they're seeking. Studies reveal that when coaches focus on the person's ideal or desired future, others are more positively motivated than when they simply problem-solve.[33] They own what they want, and that's very self-reinforcing. Your role as a leader who coaches is to anchor the conversation in their stated goals and then step aside to support their process.

> When Marco first came into Shanna's office, it seemed like he was there to vent about his last interaction with a valued customer. Marco was frustrated and felt stuck. Rather than let the conversation go down the path of how challenging the customer was, Shanna interrupted and said, "Sounds like a really tough conversation for you, Marco. Thanks for stopping by. What would you like out of our time today?"
>
> Marco stopped and looked up, suddenly aware that he'd been immersed in reliving his experience. "I'm not sure. Maybe I just want to know how I could've done it better. How could I have created a more positive interaction with my customer?" Now Shanna had a direction. She understood what mattered to Marco, and he did too.
>
> As Shanna continued her coaching, she focused on Mark's purpose: being more positive with his customer. "In the best of worlds, what would a positive outcome with this client look like, Marco?"
>
> "Well, we wouldn't have gone round and round with 'yes buts.'" Marco sighed and then brightened up. "We would've defined what the

problem really was and the best way to solve it." He paused. "I just kept getting stuck in my client's anger and didn't help him move on to how I could help him. Looking back, I felt blamed and became defensive."

"So, if we focused in the next thirty minutes on how you could step out of being defensive and help your customer focus on his problem and how you could help him, would that be valuable?" Shanna asked.

Marco replied, "Yes, that would be incredibly helpful!"

Discuss Accountability

When and how do you bring up accountability? If you've created clear expectations about the purpose of coaching and your role, accountability should be built in. As coaching becomes part of your leadership practice, others will understand that accountability remains with them. The next step is to clarify that coaching is the focus, usually at the beginning of the conversation. You might begin by saying, "I'm happy to help; I see this as a coaching opportunity—are you good with that?" Throughout the PASN Roadmap, you have an opportunity to check in with the person you're coaching about progress and direction. Ultimately, they're accountable for whatever they decide to do.

Create a Safe Space

Creating a safe space to explore, try, fail, and learn is vital to coaching. When the leader is present and shows up as nonjudgmental and willing to help, others are more willing to take risks to stretch and change. They're less likely to be fearful that their action steps and follow-through plan will set them up to fail rather than succeed.

However, leaders are so accustomed to driving accountability that it can be challenging to trust that the person they're coaching will be accountable for creating their way forward. Resist the urge to step in and give the right answer. Resist the urge to nonverbally communicate displeasure, shock, or an expression that says, "You did what?" Stick with active listening and encouragement until the right questions emerge to help the person see or experience their situation differently. When people are accepted and relaxed, their brains can search to find creative solutions and new insights. The idea of being accountable for one's plan and actions isn't tainted by "How do I please my boss?" or "What does he want me to do?"

Action Steps and Obstacles

As you check in with the other person to see if they're making progress on their issue, you'll naturally move to strategizing.

In his conversation with Shanna, Marco offered several ways he could approach his customer differently. He was most excited about turning the conversation into one where he was coaching and helping the customer.

Shanna said, "You've talked about several ways to approach a difficult conversation with a client. What would make a real difference for you and the client?"

Marco replied, "Two things. First, I'd like to focus on what they want out of the conversation right at the beginning. Second, I need to listen better to what's behind the call and how they feel. I know that I get defensive when someone blames my team or me, especially when I think they're wrong. It's not about being right, is it? And being defensive feels awful. I don't need to defend something I don't think was our fault. I need to focus on what they need so we can resolve the situation."

"Which one would you like to set in motion first?" Shanna asked. "What are the opportunities to do so?" Shanna fostered accountability by helping Marco define the specific action that would change the situation for him.

Marco thought for a moment and then said, "I think backing down, listening, and helping my client focus on what they want would work well. I have a couple of calls this week with clients, and I'll begin with this approach."

Shanna said, "Sounds like you have several opportunities this week to focus on listening to what your customer wants. How will you know when you're successful?"

Marco responded quickly, "I'll be successful if I manage my defensiveness and engage my client in a conversation where I listen, ask good questions, and the customer tells me what they need."

Leaders as Accountability Partners

When you're coaching as a leader, there's a delicate balance between respecting that the person you're coaching has defined and owned their action steps and your desire to support them in being successful. When you offer support, it's important that they define what support means. Is it simply being there if they need to talk again? Is it providing a resource they request? As you continue to empower others in your coaching, also acknowledge the impact of your presence. Understand that the person or team being coached is well aware that they're making a commitment to change and that they're making it in your presence. Finally, when they state their specific intentions out loud, they've made a significant step to owning their plan and are motivated to follow through.

The coaching conversation is both an implicit and explicit contract to help the other person reach a goal and grow. We're partnering with those we coach—walking along the path with them to offer encouragement, help them see obstacles, and define where they want to go. We're also partners in creating self-accountability.

When Accountability in Coaching Fails

When you're coaching to develop someone, avoid the following pitfalls:

- **Rushing Action Steps.** You don't want to push the person to come up with a strategy that isn't well considered or doesn't support the outcome. It's important to help them test the ideas they generate. Help them imagine the impact on themselves or others. Explore the likelihood that they're ready to take that step.
- **Taking on Too Big of a Step.** Change usually happens in small steps. If Marco wants to begin conversations by being curious

about the client's needs, he may be most successful by generating a couple of questions that would start him off. However, if his expectation is that he'll never get defensive or that he'll find several opportunities a day to change his behavior, he may be setting himself up for failure. As a coach, Shanna can help Marco identify what may work for him. She can ask him what changes he's confident he can make.

- **Inserting Your Accountability Needs.** Keep your expectations and needs for performance separate from the coaching conversation. As soon as you interject your solution, your strategy, and your need to know how it turns out, you've taken the ball of accountability from the person and stopped coaching. It might feel easier to tell them the right answer, but it won't be as successful—either in the short term or the long run.

The Self-Fulfilling Prophecy of Accountability

Accountability in coaching is a personal decision to create a plan that's successful. It's a choice, not an explicit expectation expressed by you, the leader, or the organization. It's psychologically more likely that when we choose to do something that promises something better and is aligned with our values and goals, our desire to move forward kicks in. We're motivated to change!

The impact accountability in coaching has on us is a self-fulfilling cycle of confidence and aspiration to tackle opportunities. I experienced this cycle when I decided to apply for my Master Certified Coaching certificate from the International Coaching Federation. Initially, I was halfhearted in my commitment. *Does it really matter?* I asked myself. My mentor coach continually reiterated to me the *why* of my decision. She kept me tuned in to the areas I identified as *needs improvement* to pass the audio recording assessment. I recorded many audio conversations of my coaching, and as I saw my coaching improve, my desire to be better and accomplish my goal strengthened.

Self-Accountability in a Group

After practicing their coaching, many leaders find themselves self-coaching, asking open-ended questions to hone in on where they're stuck or what they could do differently. As a result, they tell themselves, "I took this on, and it worked. Now I can take the next step and eventually reach my goal and commitment to myself."

When you coach yourself or others, you naturally foster *self-efficacy,* a term coined by Albert Bandura, a Stanford psychology professor who studied the power of beliefs and modeling in learning. Bandura's research showed that when a person believes in their capacity to execute and attain specific performance goals, they're more likely to tackle challenging situations. They're also more likely to recover from failure. Imagine leading a team or group where everyone has that experience of self-efficacy and mutual accountability!

When you coach as a leader, you're facilitating a process where others define what they want to achieve and design how they want to get there. The coaching process creates both self-accountability and self-efficacy. Motivated to follow up on what they've considered and chosen, the people you coach won't depend on you to create expectations or standards. You've empowered them to do that for themselves.

NEXT

- In your next conversation, when your help has been requested, ask a question that enables them to define and focus on what's important to them to change (see Appendix A).
- When you're grappling with an issue and begin to feel a resolution in yourself, challenge yourself to be specific about the steps you will take next.
- Focus on helping yourself and others to be clear (not dictatorial)— clear about outcomes as you imagine a compelling future.

12

SEEK COACHABLE MOMENTS

"This very moment is the perfect teacher."

—Pema Chödrön

WHEN WE WORK with leaders who are just starting to coach, they're convinced that coaching will take time and impede their ability to get things done. They believe that, like professional coaches, coaching is for formal 1-2-1 meetings, specifically designated for coaching conversations. However, unlike professional coaches, leaders have ample opportunities to coach others every day in a variety of settings. They learn to recognize coachable moments.

The benefit of being a leader who coaches is that your skills and mindset can help you be more effective throughout your leadership day. As you practice, the opportunities multiply. Your confidence grows, and coaching becomes more natural and integrates into your approach to your world.

In the first *Leaders Who Coach: Essentials* program, delivered to a group of leaders in the same organization, we discovered that leaders in any work environment can discover coachable moments.

Leaders in a wood product manufacturing company with one hundred years of tradition seemed unlikely to adopt coaching. We were forewarned that their go-to style was leading by know-how and command-and-control. Yet they wanted to learn new ways. They were integrating new generations with diverse backgrounds and talents to fit their changing industry. Their leadership, they realized, needed new tools.

From the beginning, these leaders were skeptical that we could teach them anything that would reduce injuries and increase production, their two top priorities. We role-played a drive-by-coaching opportunity. Someone who was having trouble completing an assignment because others were not getting back to her stopped a leader in the hallway. In five minutes, the leader had responded with empathy ("It's tough when people don't call you back"), encouragement ("I value your collaboration skills and drive to finish the project"), and coaching questions ("If you were your peers, at this point, what would you need to engage in your project? What's getting in your way?"). Finally, the short coaching session ended with action steps ("I appreciate you letting me know about this issue. When are you going to initiate your plan? If there's any way I can support you, let me know.").

The group acknowledged that coaching seemed to work because the manager didn't take on the problem, and the person being coached had a reasonable plan. They realized that coaching might take five to ten minutes, not thirty minutes. As they learned and practiced coaching skills and followed a coaching roadmap, they had flashes of confidence in their coaching. Still, they were skeptical—how would coaching work back in the plant, given the equipment breakdowns, emergencies, and pressure of manufacturing?

In the follow-up webinars, they shared successes and frustrations, and they continued to practice. Slowly, they recognized that coaching was an effective leadership hat. Their coaching moments multiplied.

    ○   *"We were just getting coffee. I went outside to check in with those who smoked. There was an urgent issue on the floor, and I stopped to use coaching."*

    ○   *"I found myself coaching my teenager in the car."*

Most importantly, when they coached in moments like these, they stimulated others to use their own ideas and strengths to solve issues. Furthermore, they walked away confident that the person would follow through on their plan. Problems were solved, and work was accomplished.

Use the Coach Approach

Start recognizing coachable moments by adopting the coach approach in your conversations. Assume that you don't know the answers. See your team as a group of resourceful professionals capable of finding solutions and moving forward. Start most conversations by listening and asking open-ended questions that discover what's going on and what others really want. Wait to offer advice or knowledge. The coaching mindset seeks to help others evolve and use their strengths.

For that moment, shed your other leadership hats. Leave behind the leader who's focused on quarterly goals or whether deadlines will be accomplished. Put aside the leader who has dozens of emails to respond to and another meeting to attend. You're here for one minute or thirty minutes to facilitate the others' growth.

The Four Steps to Engaging in Coachable Moments

Step I—Keep the coaching mindset top of mind.

Remaining curious and in a state of inquiry is not always easy. You might find that your mind often wanders. Begin with a coaching mindset and remember to:

- Be open to possibilities.

- Listen to what others are asking (often hidden underneath the words they're saying).
- See interactions as opportunities to grow.
- Leave behind the urge to tell others the answers, educate them, or shoot from the hip.
- Transition into being curious about the other person's agenda and needs.

Step II—Recognize the coachable moments.

Coachable moments occur when you're interacting with someone and notice that they're directly or indirectly asking you for help, a solution, etc. When you sense or hear that request, stop reacting and start listening. Leaders frequently tell us they must mindfully turn their attention to the other person and put on their coaching hat. For example, you might find yourself in the following situations:

- In the break room or lunchroom
- Walking somewhere
- Talking to a customer with a complaint or problem
- In a car traveling to a meeting with someone
- In the hallway
- In a meeting as a peer or leader
- In a group/team approaching a project or problem

Any of these everyday examples can turn into coachable moments when you're ready for coaching! All you need to do is recognize them.

Step III—Engage in coaching as you and others are ready.

As a leader who coaches, you have to be available. If you're not ready and available, it's not a good time for coaching. It's okay to notice when you're rushed, thinking about something else, depleted emotionally, or consumed with another problem. It's also okay to let someone know that now isn't a good time. Listen briefly to the request, then set a time that will work for both of you. The alternative is that you don't show up mentally. Trust me, people can tell when you're not there—and unfortunately, that experience can erode their trust in you and discourage them from reaching out for help again.

How do you know when someone is available for a coaching conversation? First, you may tune into a need or issue they're presenting in a conversation, but they haven't asked you for coaching. This is a great time to reflect back to them what you're hearing. Then you can ask them if they'd like to be coached. Identifying your time limits (if you have them) may be helpful at that time.

When you sense a coaching moment, ask yourself these questions:

- What's going on with this person?
- How are they seeing things?
- What's emerging as the purpose of the conversation for them? (There's a reason—dig a little as you seek to understand.)
- In this situation, is developing or empowering the other person to find their path appropriate?
- Is this person open to the opportunity?

Margo noticed that two people on her team were talking a great deal, and it wasn't about their assigned projects. She was annoyed—were they gossiping, wasting time, etc.? Then she remembered not to assume. What else might be going on? As she approached them, Margo smiled, sat down, and offered an observation. "You both seem very engaged in something. How's it going?"

They were surprised. They looked at each other, then slowly revealed a mutual problem they were having with the IT system. Margo engaged the coaching process by first asking them what outcome they were looking for. They shared that they needed more available support and expertise and less fear that their lack of knowledge was being judged by IT.

Margo listened carefully as she guided the conversation toward ideas and solutions they could choose to move forward with. She ended the conversation by asking if there was any way she could support them. The whole interaction took about ten minutes.

Even if a person is upset, coaching can encourage them to name their feelings and explore what those feelings mean. Functional MRI scans on our brains have shown that naming feelings engage our frontal cortex, which is responsible for analysis and decision-making.[34] Sometimes, listening and asking a few questions to help the person focus is enough. Perhaps this is followed by a heavy dose of encouragement. At other times, you can initiate a full coaching process because the person is motivated and wants to resolve a more complex or emotional issue.

Drive-By Coaching

How often does someone stop you in the hallway and begin talking about a problem, idea, or need? Are you a leader who manages by walking around—mindfully visiting other offices, sitting down next to someone to check in, or engaging with others in a break room?[35] Management by walking around continues to be a valued leadership strategy. When you informally connect with your team members, it's a chance to show them that you're curious and caring. Time with a leader is a valued commodity. Sure, they may ask you questions that need answers; often, however, they just want you to hear them.

Drive-by coaching consists of spontaneous, short moments (not more than ten minutes) when others are seeking help, direction, or a solution. There are four steps for making the most of a drive-by coachable moment:

1. Keep your coach approach mindset top of mind. Be curious and listen. Know what that feels like in your body and brain.
2. Check out what the person wants and determine if they're coachable.
3. Engage with where they'd ideally like to go in the conversation.
4. Follow the PASN Roadmap, focusing on clarifying and helping the person explore and make choices.

Coachable Moments as Collaboration

As the research shows, coaching increases collaboration.[36] We were surprised and pleased when leaders began to share that coaching resulted in more collaboration with peers, customers, and vendors. When coaching spreads throughout an organization, people naturally invite others into a conversation where everyone listens, asks exploratory questions, and focuses on the outcomes they want. It's as if coaching provides a structure for a conversation that empowers everyone to bring their thoughts, even if the situation is a conflict.

When the coach approach is used to collaborate, people are more likely to partner and make agreements about how each person will contribute to the solution. The climate of safety, listening, and inquiry creates a sense that "we're in this together."

Planned Coaching Opportunities

A key question for leaders who want to coach is: "How often do you make time to develop your team?" They often say, "Well, probably not enough." Or they might say, "Sometimes when we have our weekly meeting. Usually, however, my team just tells me how their projects are going and asks me for clarification."

No doubt, as a leader you must focus on tasks, strategies, and tactics. Just as important, however, is providing space and coaching to help others grow and realize their potential.

You can create coaching opportunities with planned meetings to develop and empower others. Make the focus of a regular 1-2-1 meeting an opportunity for a team member to come prepared to explore a topic of their choosing or plan their developmental goals.

When I consulted and coached for HP and IBM, I marveled at how important it was to those companies for leaders to schedule regular 1-2-1 meetings with their direct reports. They understood two things: 1) creating a trusting, open relationship with leaders required time set aside, and 2) the team member was asked to determine much of the agenda, which centered around their personal and career growth and development.

In the well-researched Blessing White's X Model of Engagement,[37] the apex, or high point, of engagement occurs only when both your organization and the individual's satisfaction are being achieved. This model defines engagement as the behaviors, relationships, and satisfaction that lead to high performance in your team. Successful leaders define what success looks like for the quarter, the year, etc., and communicate clear performance expectations to their team members about their role. The engagement gap is the forgotten conversation. What does your team want out of their roles, their lives, and their organization? How can they deploy their strengths and continue to grow? What would their best day look like?

The regular development conversation is an ideal time to wear your coaching hat and help others plot their life journeys. Focus on not only what's meaningful to the organization but what's meaningful to them. Then the motivation to strive and achieve is ignited and sustained. When the intersection of these two markers of engagement isn't clear, engagement deteriorates. High-performing team members tend to leave and go where they can grow.

Pete, an executive director of a nonprofit organization, was leading a pivot of his organization during the pandemic that was innovative and destined to change how they'd sustain themselves in the future. Pete was excited. Then his coach asked him, "How will these changes affect you personally? What impact will they have on your goals and personal needs?"

Pete's answer was clear. It was time for him to spend more time working on the business and less time on the day-to-day. It was time to stop working every day of the week and delegate work to other leaders and their teams. It was time to prevent burnout and take care of himself. It was time to support others to do the same. If their pivot was smart, they could retain their team and work smarter to reach their goals.

When you initiate these conversations, you may be reluctant to ask questions about someone's personal life. Yet most employees welcome your genuine interest. Try questions like these:

- Where do you see yourself in three to five years?
- What strengths do you have, and what strengths are you developing?
- What steps are you taking to achieve your goals?
- What support do you need from this organization?

You can also designate a meeting (monthly, quarterly) to develop members of your team. For this meeting, there's no other agenda. Both you and the person understand that they provide the agenda for developmental purposes. You agree on a few questions, and then the rest is coaching.

- What's going well for you right now?
- What's your vision for your life and career? How is your current role helping you get there?
- What are your challenges, and would you like to be coached on any of them?
- How can I support you?

The Crisis/Conflict Opportunity

Finally, coachable moments emerge from a conflict or crisis moment when a conversation is imperative to minimize damage or influence the direction of a negative situation. These moments initially may seem like an opportunity to tell the person what you see and what's needed now. However, often the coach approach may be effective and appropriate—it's an opportunity to coach the person to discover the real issue and own what they need to resolve the situation.

Kristy had been working as The Kids Place development director for five years. She worked fifty to sixty hours a week coordinating events and was under constant pressure to bring in more funds—every dollar made it possible for the nonprofit to provide more services. It was wearing her down. Kristy absolutely loved the nonprofit's mission, but her life had changed. She was now in a committed relationship, and she wasn't taking care of herself. One day she lost her temper at a colleague who was challenging her budget figures. "Are you kidding me? I'm doing everything I can to bring in what we need. What are you doing?" And then she stormed out of the room.

Jeff, the COO of The Kids Place, stopped by Kristy's office later and asked if she wanted to talk. Kristy apologized, but Jeff dug further to discover the stress and discouragement that was underneath her outburst.

"So, Kristy, it sounds like you feel drained, and the excitement for your position is mostly gone," Jeff said.

"I guess that's true," Kristy admitted. "I hate to say it, though. I love The Kids Place. We do so much good here."

"Your commitment to our mission remains, Kristy. The role, not so much. So, I wonder if you'd be open to exploring what might be a better fit for you right now—even if it's not with us," Jeff said.

Kristy looked up, surprised. "Sure. I need to continue working, and I don't want to leave. I love our mission."

"So, tell me, Kristy," Jeff replied. "Have you been daydreaming at all about what you'd like to do now? What do you want to change? What does spark your interest?"

Kristy quickly said, "I can tell you what doesn't!"

"Okay, let's start there," Jeff said calmly.

"Our events take it out of me. I'd like to not do them. I like being on the leadership team, and I don't want to be the person responsible for the engine that keeps the organization going."

Jeff said, "What else?"

Kristy paused and then said, "I love kids, and I haven't used my social work background at all. Sometimes I wonder what I could do so I could be closer to the kids and our programs. That's a cool idea."

Jeff said, "I noticed that your energy really picked up when you started talking about our kids. Tell me more about how you could use your strengths and get your energy back."

Jeff recognized that Kristy's outburst came from a place that deserved exploration and possibly coaching. It was a coachable moment because Kristy wanted to talk, and her emotions were stopping her from exploring what she needed. Jeff also recognized that a burned-out leader falls short of her potential, and the organizational needs eventually suffer. He was willing to start with where Kristy was and help her figure out where she might rejuvenate and give more to the organization.

Coachable moments emerge from the leader's confidence in their ability to coach when others want to share, have a problem to be solved, or need support and encouragement. These moments become the story of how the organization thrives.

Like life, coaching often happens in moments, not events. We string each moment together to become our stories. When we started the *Leaders Who Coach: Essentials* program, we wondered how coaching would fit in with busy leaders who wore multiple hats. Our leaders who coached showed us that once they understood the power of coaching and made it their own, coachable moments became a reliable leadership skill. It was interwoven into their core values and approach to leading others.

NEXT

- Make a list of the times you might like to be coached. Then turn it around and imagine all the places others might want to be coached. Start looking for coachable moments there.
- Reflect on the coachable moments you've coached. Then make a list of the moments you could have coached someone in the last week.
- Consider scheduling regular meetings to develop others. Come up with three regular questions to get started. Communicate the purpose of the meetings and ask participants to experiment with you.

COACH TO IMPROVE
PERFORMANCE

"We cannot solve problems with the same thinking that created them."

—Albert Einstein

HOW USEFUL IS coaching when someone needs to improve their performance? This question plagues leaders because, eventually they are accountable to stakeholders, their boss etc. for the overall performance of their team. They don't want to shirk their responsibility. As we show in this chapter, coaching can enhance your ability to help your team to improve their performance. Assessing *when* and *how* to coach are the better questions to ask.

Defining Performance: It's Not Just What You Do; It's How You Do It

When you measure performance, you compare the desired results versus actual results. There are two parts: what you desire and how the person or the team achieves those results.

As we discuss in the chapter on accountability, alignment on clear outcomes and expectations is a basic prerequisite to achieving agreement on the *what* of results. How do we measure it? Sales, retention of customers, products created, services rendered, completion of tasks, value of contribution—the possible measurements are unlimited because they're directly related to your industry, your company's mission, and your expectations of your team. Suffice it to say, without the clear alignment of measured results, it's easy for misunderstanding, failure, and frayed relationships to occur.

Concurrently, there's *how* an individual and the team achieve results. The *how* is sometimes more critical than the *what*. Everyone is familiar with the executive who browbeats his team to churn out quarterly numbers, with the spillover of poor morale, low retention, and burnout. How people perform is more than numbers—it involves ethics, values, and relationships. For example, what are the expectations of your culture or core values? Did the person achieve the results by themselves, or did they collaborate with others? Did their style or methods meet the standards and values you set? Did they create obstacles and problems for those around them? These, too, are performance issues.

The need for performance improvement can lie in the gap between what was achieved and what was expected by the organization. It can also be defined by the gap between a person or team's expectations of themselves—which may be different and beyond the expectations of the organization—and the results. When the leader and the individual are clear on the gap, the viability of coaching is strong. In other words, when you and your team member agree on what needs improvement, coaching can accelerate growth and help close the gap.

Trends in Performance Appraisal Favor Coaching

During the last ten years, companies large and small have realized that their traditional yearly performance appraisal process did far more harm than good. The shift in performance management has been from appraisal to learning. More than one-third of large companies have thrown out their traditional performance appraisals in favor of frequent check-ins.

By emphasizing individual accountability for past results, traditional appraisals give short shrift to improving current performance and developing talent for the future. That can hinder long-term competitiveness.[38]

In addition, even high performers tend to be demotivated by the traditional performance appraisal process. The anxiety of preparing to hear how you've been doing over the last year creates unnecessary stress and anxiety.

Moving to an informal system requires a culture of continuous developmental feedback—a way to support the person as they learn and evolve. These days, organizations are significantly more concerned about how their employees reach their goals. Assessing applicants and team members on core values has become integral to hiring and developing team members. Coaching skills are essential in those conversations that focus on the demonstration of values, integrity, and culture.

There are three common situations where improving performance emerges for leaders and their teams. Which one you use depends on who drives the performance issues. They include the Top-Down Approach, the Coaching-to-Improve Conversation, and the Joint Accountability Collaboration. As a leader, you may initiate all three of these when the situation's appropriate.

The Top-Down Approach

When organizations and leaders drive everything from the top down, there tends to be a limited opportunity to use coaching. Communication is one way and only open to questions, not collaboration.

- Here's what you accomplished or didn't do . . .
- Here's what you did well . . .
- Here's what you need to improve/do differently . . .
- Here are my suggestions . . .
- Here's your rating/ranking . . .
- Any questions?

Scenario #1: Jorge recognizes that there's a pattern in Daniel's performance. He produces a great product, but he usually takes too long or is late. Jorge also has heard complaints from others on the team about the impact of Daniel's past-due pattern. They depend on his information to build their part of the proposal. They feel rushed to complete the proposal and are growing resentful that Daniel isn't improving.

Daniel knows these complaints are true. He prepares himself for yet another conversation with his boss about how he could do quality work in less time. He feels bad, but he doesn't know how to do things differently.

Since Jorge has discussed the matter with Daniel before, he decides to put him on a ninety-day improvement plan. "Daniel, the analysis you provide for our proposals is outstanding. The problem, as you know, is that you take too long to produce it." Daniel nods, hanging his head a bit. "Because our clients expect an on-time delivery, we all must follow through with our internal agreements. I've decided to create a ninety-day plan to improve your timeliness."

Daniel looks discouraged. "I've tried to do it in less time, but it doesn't fit my standards. I guess I'm a perfectionist," he explains.

Jorge replies, "Sounds like you may be so focused on a perfect product that it gets in the way of being good enough to pass on to others. I know you're trying. Let's figure out a game plan to turn your projects in earlier. Maybe I can review them a week before they're due and give feedback. In the meantime, I'd like to refer you to our Employee Assistance Program to identify what it would take to address your perfectionism or whatever's getting in the way. How does that sound?"

In this case, Jorge is driving the conversation all the way. He's compassionate and willing to provide resources, and he recognizes Daniel's strengths. Yet he's not interested in Daniel's perspective or ideas about what it might take to change. Without that input, Daniel isn't likely to succeed. Then what?

The top-down-only approach to improving performance is quickly fading as it tends to alienate new generations entering the workplace. Leaders and organizations now recognize that a two-way conversation, with joint ownership of both the issue and solution, is far more effective, regardless of that person's generation.

The Coaching-to-Improve Conversation

When leaders coach consistently, their teams soon realize that they're available to help them with challenging situations. They feel they can safely share, "I screwed this up, and I'd like to learn how to do this better next time," without jeopardizing their career or credibility. In fact, in a culture that values development and growth, acknowledging opportunities for do-overs can be perceived as a strength.

In this type of culture, everyone has a habit of defining what they want to do or how they want to be better. They have the autonomy to control or influence how they'll achieve goals for themselves, and the organization greatly affects their motivation to strive and change. When your team member or colleague tells you what they want to change, it's relatively easy to step in and coach them. The follow-through to change rests primarily with the person because they've owned the issue from the beginning. The person generates self-accountability, and the leader can adopt a purer coach approach. It's more of a bottom-up approach. As with 1-2-1 conversations, the leader begins coaching with more challenging questions.

- What would you like to improve or change?
- How can you better use your strengths in this situation?
- In what areas would you like to contribute more?
- What goals would you like to set?

These questions become increasingly more specific as the person being coached defines the improvements or changes they'd like to make. Once again, the leader doesn't have an agenda of "you need to change or improve."

> *Scenario #2: Jorge recognizes that Daniel is a valued member of his team, even if team members are frustrated by his timing. When Daniel brings up the issue of his tardiness, Jorge encourages him to focus on an outcome he wants by asking, "What would a better outcome look like to you?"*
>
> *Daniel thinks carefully and says, "Well, I'd like to produce the same quality and be on time so my analysis can support my team."*
>
> *Jorge acknowledges that they agree on that goal. He clarifies what "same quality" means and then asks, "Was there ever a time you were able to do that?"*
>
> *Daniel thinks for a moment and then recounts a time three months ago when he knew the analysis was good enough to send along. Jorge drills down into Daniel's self-expectations and encourages him to consider what the team needs. "Could you be expecting more than the team actually needs?" Finally, Jorge asks, "What do you need to know to make sure the quality was good enough?"*
>
> *Daniel looks up and says, "I'd need you or someone on the team to give me feedback along the way."*
>
> *Together, Jorge and Daniel create a specific plan and timelines for what that change might look like.*

Joint Accountability

What's the role of coaching when performance is substandard, and you're responsible for addressing and initiating a conversation about it? Once you deliver feedback to your team member about the gap between your expectations and how they're performing, there's an opportunity to have a conversation about how the team member hears it. Do you both see it the same way?

A joint accountability conversation begins with agreeing on the specific target for improvement. As a leader, you're clear about your expectations, and you initiate a frank conversation about the gap between results and expectations. It can also arise from in-the-moment discussions about what's gone awry from both your and your team members' perspectives. In joint accountability conversations, both the leader and the person they're coaching are invested in the results. As a result, there's joint ownership and accountability. Here are specific coaching questions that may facilitate the joint accountability conversation:

- What do you see as your strengths and areas of improvement?
- What was your most significant accomplishment this year?
- What skills do you have that we're not utilizing?
- Where's your biggest opportunity to contribute more?
- My perspective on what you could do to improve your performance is . . . What's your perspective?
- Now that we agree on what's most important for you to improve, what help do you need to create an improvement plan?

When you, as a leader, share accountability with your team or team member, each person must enter the situation with clear intentions, values, and openness.

- They agree to the core values and specific goals.
- The leader's clear about what they own and what's jointly owned.
- The leader defines the *what* and coaches *how* the person might improve.
- The team member agrees to own their performance improvement goals.
- Both leader and team member are willing to listen to each other, as well as give candid feedback to ensure true agreement.
- Once agreement and clarity are achieved, the leader uses the coach approach and the coaching roadmap.

The final aspect of joint accountability is defining each one's role and the action steps each will take when a plan is in place.

Scenario #3: Jorge provides Daniel with the following feedback: "When I read your reports, I notice that they're incredibly detailed. As we've discussed, Daniel, the team needs less detail in your reports and more on-time performance. We have a big project coming up next month, so it's important that the whole team be on time. What are your plans to provide less detail and deliver on time on this project?"

Once they agree on the goals, Jorge continues to coach, as he did in Scenario #2. In addition, he suggests regular check-ins to support Daniel's confidence that his report will meet the needs of the team while knowing he can provide additional resources if needed.

Your coaching can transform a performance management conversation or an improved performance conversation into a shared *we* dynamic rather than a *me-as-leader* dynamic. You elicit your team member's perspectives, strengths, and ultimate buy-in because they, not you, will be following through on the identified action steps. If they create or co-create those steps with you, they're more likely to understand them and be self-accountable. Once again, as a leader who coaches, you assume that the person you're coaching can identify the answers and resources they need to change. Whether improving performance is about what your team members do or how they do it, your coaching invites them into a compelling conversation about how to be successful.

NEXT

- Identify an opportunity to meet with a team member with the goal of performance improvement. Initiate a clear conversation about the gap between performance and expectations.
- Check for agreement on what needs to change. Adopt the coach approach by encouraging the person to identify what and how they want to change.
- Employ coaching skills throughout your conversation.
- Use the PASN Roadmap and help them identify specific steps they'll take to reach their goal.

14

THE COACH APPROACH TO UNLEASHING TEAM GENIUS

"No longer do the main challenges in organizations lie in the people or in the parts but in the interfaces and relationships between people, teams, functions, and different stakeholder needs."

—Peter Hawkins

THROUGHOUT THIS BOOK, you've read examples of coaching individuals as well as teams. One of the most surprising and fulfilling results of working with the hundreds of leaders who've adopted a coach approach is observing how they use it. Examples include:

- Environmental leaders gathering a community to collaborate on a project

- Parents using a coach approach with children who are surprisingly open to solving issues themselves
- Customers who need help defining what they want from the business
- Teams looking for a way to define a problem and solve it by leveraging all strengths and ideas in the room

When you realize that your purpose as a leader, parent, or peer who coaches is helping others to develop their own path for going forward, your coach approach becomes a way to empower the world.

How Individual and Team Coaching Differ

Most leaders are constantly striving to create a team that's cohesive, interdependent, and capable of moving forward together, without the leader constantly needing to guide the interactions. In team coaching, you focus on the whole team rather than individuals. Your coaching helps the team reflect on their dynamic and listen to their many voices. What's everyone hearing from one another? What are the goals or issues they're focusing on?

As a leader who coaches, you become a mirror for the team, actively listening to what the group is saying and asking the entire group powerful questions. You realize that your input as a leader is one of many voices. You're constantly reinforcing the interdependency of the team; that is, the team leverages everyone's input and voice to accomplish the best results. There's collective responsibility and accountability to one another and a recognition that the team has a shared fate.

Previously, we mentioned the example of the software development leader who had a constant stream of developers in his office whenever they felt stuck. He recognized that they were more technologically current and thus better prepared to solve the problem than he was. When he became a leader who coaches, he backed off from the role they'd thrust upon him and started to coach the group. His model is a great template for coaching a small group:

1. He ignored the invitation to solve the problem and instead countered with, "Help me understand the outcome you want from our conversation." Once the issues were identified, the outcome became clearer.
2. Then he responded, "Let's first identify the real issues here." He asked coaching questions such as, "When did you feel stuck? How did you respond? What's holding you back?" His team used the whiteboard to illustrate. What they landed on wasn't what they thought would be the focus.
3. The group strategized. The developers, not the leader, continued to illustrate possible solutions on the whiteboard. They fed off one another's insight and leapfrogged to solutions that might work.
4. The leader was careful to help them summarize their milestones and the challenges they identified. Questions such as "How might this not work?" and "Why?" came up many times.
5. At the end, the leader asked them to reiterate the plan and how they would test what they were going to do next.

From that moment forward, groups that came to his office jumped into the process of identifying the real issue automatically. Expecting their leader to be a coach became the norm. In the process, they learned to ask open-ended questions, and their respect for one another's knowledge and experience grew. They understood that, together, they could solve the issue.

You can also teach the coaching process to your team in the following ways:

- If you're coaching them individually, use that experience as a bridge. Together you can share and discuss the steps in coaching you've used (Identify, Ascertain, Strategize, Next).
- Enroll them to be your co-coaches. Help them understand the power of *how* and *what* questions to discover solutions within the team.
- Once an issue or goal statement is clarified, you can move through the PASN Roadmap.

- Whiteboards, flip charts, and visual aids are important to represent the group's wisdom and thoughts. Our brain has different channels for audio and visual input, and when we use both, we improve our ability to analyze, learn, and remember.
- As in individual coaching, when you coach a team, strategies will emerge once you explore the issue or goal. Invite participants to write down and post their ideas (using sticky notes and flip charts). Writing down the thoughts that are shared is a great strategy to discourage groupthink and encourage diverse input. Then you can begin to discuss the themes and merits of each.
- Finally, create an action plan. Who's responsible for what, and by when? How will success be measured, and what does the group anticipate that may get in the way?
- As a leader who coaches, your role is to keep the process on track, reflect, encourage, and keep asking probing questions that uncover the obstacles and best ideas.

Are you getting the picture? Can you imagine the whole group involved in a conversation in which everyone feels responsible for an outcome using the best ideas in the room? That's what you can create when you coach a team or group.

Like individual coaching, team coaching is only appropriate when you want the group to be involved in the process. Be clear about the extent to which you're empowering your team to decide—on the issues, on the solutions, on the accountability. Are you telling them what you're going to do? Selling them on an idea? Testing your decision? Only seeking input? Or do you have faith in your team to co-create where you're going and how?[39] While coaching skills can facilitate a group conversation at each level of team involvement, it's when you're ready to empower your team to tackle an entire issue and outcome that coaching's most effective. It's your decision—just be up front about it.

Linda was the executive director of a nonprofit that served families throughout the state. Four locations operated in several cities, but each location felt like walking into a different culture. The lack of consistency in culture was causing problems in communication and delivery of services, so Linda met with her leadership team that represented the different locations.

"I need your help," she began. "I've heard from most of you that the communication between our offices isn't going well. People show up late for Zoom meetings. We don't agree on how to measure success, and we don't seem to appreciate one another. I sense that these are symptoms of deeper issues. I think we provide a wonderful service to others, yet I can't help believing that we could do so much better if we addressed these issues. Are you willing to work with me to figure out what's going on and what we can change?"

They all nodded. Linda facilitated the conversation that followed, writing down thoughts and ideas on a flip chart as they emerged. Then she asked, "What stands out to you as the core issues?"

The team agreed that they spent little time getting to know one another across locations. They spent so much time on their clients, they'd failed to create a culture across the agency that was supportive, respectful, and aligned. Furthermore, they acknowledged that, as the leadership team, they didn't fully hash out their disagreements in strategy, and this led to different processes.

Linda reflected these issues back to the team and then asked, "How can we best address our observations and experiences? What do you want?" The rest of the meeting focused on the team's goals, along with immediate steps they could take and a long-range plan to change how they related and did business internally. Linda's willingness to ask her team for help and to empower them with the coach approach led to an open, candid discussion and the motivation to change—together.

To be a leader, you must have people who follow you. No leader can accomplish the mission alone. No team can be effective unless it's interdependent and serves a common mission. When you coach your team, you strengthen your team's collective ability to accomplish results.

The Universality of the Coach Approach

Whatever team or organizational principles you follow, being a leader who coaches is an advantage. As we stated at the beginning of this book, coaching's not an end in itself; it's a means to an end. It's a way to focus on the right issues and foster collaboration for results. Our leaders have reported that coaching supports other organizational structures and principles they've adopted. Here are two examples:

1. Many of the businesses with whom I work have implemented the Entrepreneur Operating System (EOS) as a way of creating values, accountability, systemic processes, and a common language for moving an organization forward.[40] In the EOS system, one of the most powerful tools for creating accountability and focusing the team is called *Level 10 Meetings*. Regular Level 10 Meetings are designed to help a leadership team create a consistent rhythm that keeps the company focused on the vision. EOS has clear guidelines for identifying, discussing, and truly solving problems. In addition to tracking and following up on action steps, the core of a great Level 10 Meeting is understanding the root of the problem and constructively solving it. One leader who coaches shared that at her Level 10 Meetings, she asked standard coaching questions such as:

   • "What's worked well, and what can we celebrate?"
   • "What's getting in the way of accomplishing the goals we've set?"
   • "What strategies do you have for addressing that issue, and what help do you want from the rest of the team?"

   As a result, her EOS Level 10 Meetings were rich in participation and new ideas.

2. Other leaders have adopted the outward mindset put forth by the Arbinger Institute. Arbinger's work equips people to understand and affect change at the mindset level. By providing

models that help us look inward and change ourselves, Arbinger facilitates cultural change, minimizes unproductive conflict, and produces dramatically better organizational results. Individuals understand the difference, learn how an inward mindset hinders relationships and results, and know how to shift to an outward mindset.[41] Here's how one leader uses coaching by applying this model:

> *We ask all employees to read* Leadership and Self-Deception. *Then we sit down with each team member to discuss what they've learned and how they might apply it to interactions in the workplace. Coaching allows me to adapt to each person's style and background. I ask about their experience and encourage them. I use a coach approach, not a teach approach, to help them share their experience and to help others decide the best way for them to begin to apply the principles. What doesn't work for them? What does? As in coaching, they're challenged to figure out how the mindset concepts apply to their behavior and figure out how the concept applies to them. Our message is that you only have control over yourself.*

Leaders have also reported that coaching customers or other stakeholders have helped others clarify their needs and create a collaborative partnership. When customers with ambiguous needs or complaints are coached, they feel listened to, and more importantly, they clarify what they need and want. Together, they forge a path forward.

Groups and Teams Who Coach One Another

Vistage is the leading CEO organization in the world. Their mission is to create a tightly bonded group of senior executives or CEOs who learn to use a modified coaching model for how peers can process issues and opportunities. They learn to ask deeper open-ended questions, hold one another accountable for commitments, and respect the choices that others make.

As a Vistage Chair for eight years, I've witnessed the power of peers accelerating one another's growth through support and coaching. I was surprised to discover peer coaching created powerful and positive accountability. Not to me—to one another. I believed that because they were in charge and responsible for leading the business and their teams, they were already accountable. Indeed, they are. However, when it comes to changing their challenging behaviors, making difficult decisions, or reaching for a brass ring that's far off, they can feel alone and unsupported because everyone in their business has their agenda. Thus, they understand that their commitment to take a step, accomplish something, and come back to share with nonjudgmental peers releases them to make decisions and take risks to grow their business. I've also observed that leaders in my group now have permission to focus on their development and learning. As a result, stress decreases, and Vistage businesses grow at least two-and-a-half times more than businesses of their peers.

What model do you use to create a culture or facilitate an effective team? Our leaders have taught us that the coaching mindset and skills strengthen their ability to lead beyond the individual. When you coach teams, you generate trust and create buy-in in your entire culture.

NEXT

- Choose a team or group to coach in the next week. Which skills do you want to practice? How will you listen better?
- Prepare an outline using the PASN Roadmap. What questions might be appropriate? Imagine yourself as a team member in the room and identify key questions you can ask to help your team identify their goal or discover what's getting in the way.
- What's your role? Be clear about what decisions you're trusting the team to make and what discretion you may have as the leader.
- Save time at the end of a team meeting to elicit feedback from the group about what went well, what didn't, and so on. What did you learn for the next time you coach your team?

15

COACHING THROUGH CHANGE, CRISIS, AND PANDEMICS

"When we are no longer able to change a situation, we are challenged to change ourselves."

—Viktor E. Frankl

ALL COACHING IS about change. As we've stated throughout this book, coaching isn't appropriate and won't be successful unless a person or team seeks to have a better or clearer future—e.g., resolve an issue, improve their performance, or create a better life. However, what if we don't choose the change? What if change chooses us?

Viktor E. Frankl's poignant quote reflects a conviction that helped him survive and find meaning from his horrific experience in the Nazi concentration camps.[42] His perspective also speaks to a core coaching principle: When we coach, we coach the person, not the situation, precisely because only that person can decide how they'll respond to the change foisted on them.

Beginning in 2020, these challenges have accelerated: the COVID-19 pandemic, economic hardship, social and racial injustice, and the Great Resignation. Even during these extraordinary times, leaders who coach have empowered others to reach inside themselves to adapt and pivot. Coaching is, after all, a conversation. "Our work, our relationships, and our lives succeed or fail one conversation at a time. While no single conversation is guaranteed to transform a company, a relationship, or a life, any single conversation can."[43] Remember that many of those who are holding down the fort in our workplaces are also part of the hidden resignation. Although they remain at work, almost half are thinking about leaving. Their energy has diminished, and they need replenishment. So when we and those around us feel battered by change we haven't chosen, remember to focus on the moment, the person, and the conversation.

The Psychology of Stress

How does coaching help cushion the impact of stress? The psychology of stress is based on the premise that we all like and seek predictability. Furthermore, we want to believe that we're in control of any change that does happen. In my graduate work, I studied the impact of the perception of control on people faced with uncontrollable environmental stress while trying to solve an unsolvable puzzle. It turns out that people's ability to persist, even on an unsolvable task, significantly increased when they *believed* they could terminate the noxious noise (stressor). Moreover, that was true even if they never stopped the stress. In other words, believing in and focusing on what we can control is an essential buffer against negative stress.

Teams and organizations are no different. When your team or company is in crisis—or, as all of us have experienced during the writing of this book, experiencing a continuous life-threatening pandemic that affects everything—our stress level and our desire to control is amplified. When our routine lives are suddenly and severely disrupted, our ability to focus and make effective choices is also disrupted. In this chapter, we explore some ways that coaching can help others successfully journey through an uncertain, disruptive time.

Relationships Matter—Use Your Coaching Skills to Connect

When we don't see that we have any choices and when we're isolated, we tend to be a captive of our feelings. Whether we're feeling despair, fear, or anger, it's easy to stay mired in our feelings. Above all, we're social animals, and we naturally long for connection and support. We want to know that we're not alone and that our feelings, though hard, are shared by other humans.

As the shock waves of the pandemic have seeped into so many facets of our lives, we and our businesses are collectively weary. We're trying to make sense of what it means to the future. What new variant is next? What will our workplaces look like? How will the supply chain issues be resolved? In this time of the Great Resignation, where will we find the people to support our growth? As Ernest Hemingway once said: "The world breaks everyone, and many are strong at the broken places." What we've learned builds resilience to carry into the future. As we've worked remotely, practiced physical distancing, and adapted to hybrid work environments, leaders are discovering that their teams are hungry to connect. Cut off from spontaneous interactions with others, they want clarity about where the business is going, and they want to know that they're contributing. They want humor and camaraderie. While spontaneous coachable moments that in the past arose from leading by walking around may have vanished, the chances to coach virtually have multiplied. Remember, coaching isn't about telling; it's about asking and listening. Here's how you can better navigate those opportunities using your coaching skills.

Themes to Coach During the Pandemic

During a prolonged social or organizational change, resist the urge to focus only on tasks in your individual and team meetings. Always check in with the well-being of all with whom you're meeting. Help normalize what others are feeling. Share your feelings, the up-and-down experiences, and the challenges of working from home. Then explore others' experiences. When people engage directly in identifying and coping with the stressor rather than minimizing or avoiding it, their health and other outcomes are significantly better. Continue to help others name emotions such as anxiety, fear, and uncertainty—as well as excitement and joy. Naming emotions will help your team gain clarity and share their humanity.

As we've mentioned in previous chapters, when you name it, you tame it. It turns out that when we label our feelings, it requires our executive functioning prefrontal cortex to engage, thus accessing our problem-solving functions. Using the Gottman Institute feeling wheel (see Appendix B) helps provide labels for feelings. There's no right label for our feelings; we get to choose. A feeling wheel provides nuanced ways to integrate feelings into our decisions and conversations. Categories under the labels *mad* and *joy* are connected to other words such as *frustrated* or *happy*. Including feeling words that many people associate with these labels enriches and increases the effectiveness of conversations about feelings.

Use your empathetic paraphrasing when you're feeling with or for others, and then use your encouragement to point out their strengths and contributions. When you listen and provide an environment to share emotions and experiences, you encourage conversation and diminish isolation. I've heard many leaders initiate conversations about emotions during these and other times.

> *Martin opened a virtual conversation with his team about the recent massive demonstrations regarding racial justice in our country. He knew it was on their mind. He simply shared his dismay about the suffering and asked aloud, "I wonder how others are reacting and feeling." He*

said most team members were open to sharing, and politics never entered the conversation. No one judged anyone else; everyone's experience was respected.

Martin then shared the company's focus on inclusion and equality and invited his team to speak to him either then or privately about their ideas or needs. He thanked everyone for sharing and assured them that the conversation wasn't over. Then they moved on to another purpose of the meeting. The conversation would continue.

In another example, associates in a law firm decided to have their own Zoom meeting, not to complain but to share what they missed (concerts, movies, restaurants, etc.). It was okay to cry, laugh, and acknowledge their human experience during COVID-19.

Remember, emotions are information, and your openness to them helps others understand what's happening and what they need or want to happen. Conversations that include emotions also can help you determine who may need additional resources or more of your attention. A basic tenet of emotional intelligence is that if you don't pay attention to emotions, they can easily derail your decisions and show up unexpectedly. That's as true on a team as it is with individuals.

What's Going to Happen Next? A Coach Approach to Messaging and Leading the Team

We're living in a hyper VUCA (volatile, uncertain, complex, and ambiguous) world. As a leader, you don't know when the COVID-19 virus will wane, when the economy might recover, or how your next quarter will look. It's easy to get lost in uncertainty. At the same time, it's wise to heed Napoleon Bonaparte's words: "The role of a leader is to define reality and give hope." How you act now will set the trajectory of your organization for many years to come.

The coach approach is about being authentic about what you don't know. You then can share what you and the organization are doing: adapting to provide safety and well-being, pivoting to create new products and services, flexing to allow different ways to work, and being open to feedback about what needs improving. You can listen and help others focus on what they want and how they can contribute to those changes. You can use the full PASN Roadmap model to rouse others to find their individual path or create a common path. A recent study by Better-Up showed that future-minded leaders that weigh positive and negative outcomes make more reasonable decisions, and they are less anxious and depressed.

The coach approach can also alleviate stress by focusing on where a person or a team ideally would like to go. Recently, researchers found that using the style of coaching for compliance, with participants focused only on what they needed to improve or overcome, left participants feeling "guilty and self-conscious." Coaching that instead focused on personal dreams and how people might achieve them elicited positive emotions and was deemed by participants to be "inspiring and caring." Neuroimaging studies show that coaching that encourages others to explore what's possible activates areas of the brain associated with openness to new ideas, change, and learning. While defining the problem has a clear role in your coaching, coaching that taps into ideal states, desires, and dreams creates a positive sense of safety that allows the people you coach to face rather than avoid difficulties.[44]

> When High Country Technology's contract prospects dropped off as a result of the pandemic, the small entrepreneurial team felt gut-punched. This was the year they expected to double their revenue. Rather than double efforts to go after their base clients, CEO Rebecca first focused on her small team's morale and vision for the future. "I know it's disappointing and a little scary to have these projects delayed. We also know that our products are needed and valued by those who use them. I'd like to spend time focusing on our future. Yes, some prospects have fallen away, yet what possibilities has this new environment opened up? What do you see?"
>
> She led the team in a discussion about a future vision that was on her back burner.
>
> "What are you feeling excited about that's new? How has our market changed? What's our biggest obstacle in this pandemic world?" Her

questions and listening began to raise the energy of her team, and together they created a new vision of where they were going and what it might take to get there. Rebecca initially generated her vision, and her coaching invited everyone on her team to design a new plan together.

As workplaces and our communities reopen in response to falling COVID-19 rates and increased vaccinations, the top question organizations are asking is, "How do we come back to work?" Manufacturing, service-facing businesses, essential workers, etc., have fewer choices. However, other companies discover that an everyone-return-on-this-date mandate creates a cacophony of feelings and opinions. As a result, leaders who coach have brought their teams together to focus on the values of the business and the needs of their team. For some, flexibility creates new freedom without diminishing performance. For others, fear of COVID-19 variants or immune vulnerabilities creates resistance. Still, others long for connection and realize that their performance is tied to being at work in person. Coaching can help leaders of every organization respond collectively to the different needs while not compromising the integrity of the business moving forward. As we have repeatedly stated, leaders who coach lead by listening empathetically and asking hard questions. As a result, awareness rises, and teams commit to a plan. Everyone understands that the world's still in flux, but there's a path forward they can get behind.

In times of crisis and pandemics, coaching conversations about impact and stress are continuous. When we're isolated and despairing, it's easy to fall into malaise and not be productive. When you coach, you acknowledge the experiences present, and you help people focus on their vision of the future and determine the next steps to get there.

Coaching During Organizational Change

Even welcomed change can be stressful. While teams may see change as positive, they can still experience loss. We've all been there—a reorganization to be more efficient, a promotion, scaling the business to grow, or simply transitioning to a new leader and being part of a new team can challenge us. We lose what has been familiar and predictable.

When you lead change, don't minimize the impact of the transition. Begin by being curious about how your team's experiencing the change. What do they perceive as the *why* of the change? Does it match what you or the organization intended? What's in it personally for them? Without awareness of purpose, those who feel resistant or fearful aren't likely to desire the direction you've set. What do they need to make the transition? What works and what won't work? Well-regarded models of change, such as the Prosci ADKAR Model, make clear that change happens one person at a time. ADKAR is an acronym for the five outcomes an individual needs to achieve for change to be successful: Awareness, Desire, Knowledge, Ability, and Reinforcement.[45] As with coaching, without addressing awareness and desire in individuals, people will resist and even sabotage change.

A large, successful technology company promoted new leadership and new plans to reorganize and segment the business. The marketing VP, Duane, dreaded the aftermath of the new CEO's announcement, which had been broadcast to everyone in the building. The disagreement and discouragement vibes were palpable to him. Usually, he'd meet his team and immediately make plans to meet the new directives. But he decided to use a coach approach instead. He set up a flip chart and said, "I understand that this announcement wasn't what many of you wanted to hear and that you and I may disagree. I'd like to spend time at this meeting identifying what you think and how you feel."

The team quickly responded with words such as disappointed, ill-advised, and other emotional words. After each input, Duane wrote the themes on the board and repeated them out loud. When they were done, he read them all again. He respected his team's perspectives. Then he challenged them and asked, "How do we implement these changes in a way that respects the values and experience of our division? What can we do to make the transition and our business successful?"

He was surprised and gratified that the group was ready to focus their energies on adapting to the challenge. They jumped in without hesitation. He wrote their ideas on the board and added a few of his own. He read those aloud too and then said, "These are great ideas. Thank you. I know it's not easy to pivot and focus on a way forward, and you have. Let's review these at our next meeting and create a compelling strategy." The team walked away united, with a sense of purpose and respect for their leader.

Later, Duane exclaimed that it was the first time he had ever received thank-you emails from his team about a meeting. They appreciated that they had a chance to say what was true for them and then focus on what they could do to shape the future.

Duane used his coaching skills to lead his team through a difficult change. He wasn't afraid to hear what he knew people were thinking and feeling. Although they weren't part of making the decision, he validated their feelings and engaged them in defining strategies for making it work.

Coaching Virtually

Meeting virtually has become ubiquitous, and it's here to stay. The pandemic made working virtually a necessity, and that necessity has turned into an accepted tool for communicating, meeting, and working with one another. In addition, many of your team members working virtually have been dividing their time between homeschooling children, taking care of parents, coordinating daily living-together tasks, and doing their jobs. For those industries that can, giving employees the choice and autonomy to work virtually has become a powerful way to retain their best team members.

Virtual coaching has plenty of psychological challenges for everyone—especially when it's a change from the way you've communicated before. Here are some virtual coaching best practices that may help you ensure that time is well spent.

Coaching Virtually Best Practices

- **Check In.** When you communicate virtually, always provide time to check in about personal well-being and share personal stories as you do in person when meetings are more spontaneous. Be open to talking about the impact of stress on sleep, health, and relationships. Virtual coaching requires that we listen better and realize that some team members are more comfortable with video and talking than others.

- **Coach for Development Now.** These moments of uncertainty and increased time alone can stimulate questions and concerns about aspirations and the future that your team members have never broached before. Paradoxically, this is a great time to have people step back and assess their career goals and opportunities. Simple questions like "What's on your mind about what's next for you at work and in your life?" can start the conversation.

- **Ensure Confidentiality.** Ask about the confidentiality of the meeting. Many working from home are using spaces such as their kitchens, living rooms, and underneath the stairwell to connect on their computer. Are they comfortable talking about difficult matters in these settings? Do they have headphones that prevent others from hearing? Consider using the chat line to converse about things that are uncomfortable to share aloud if the space isn't entirely secure.

- **Master the Virtual Platform.**
  o Adjust your camera so that the person sees more of you (be further away) and make sure your audio is clear. When we see more body language, communication is more complete, and emotions are clearer.
  o Use the assortment of tools provided by your virtual platform. Sharing a whiteboard or Word document to write down themes or issues could bring a depth to your coaching that you don't get in person. Allow others to share their documents and videos.

- o If you're coaching a group, ask that everyone share their video, so they can be seen by all when you are conversing. The interaction is less effective and counterproductive when some are seen on camera and others aren't. Not using video also provides the space for them to get distracted with something else. In addition, establish ground rules about not working on emails or looking at phones unless there's a compelling reason. Finally, in large groups, ask everyone to stay muted unless it's their turn to talk to avoid background noise.
- o Consider that individual meetings can decrease in effectiveness after forty-five minutes for individuals and ninety minutes for a group. Our eyes (which don't blink enough on Zoom) typically defocus, and our brains become tired. Finally, videos can also be stressful because we worry about how we look to others. Play with ways to defuse the focus on how we look.
- **Keep Your 1-2-1 Meetings.** Whether virtual or in person, consistently schedule your one-on-one meetings and perhaps increase them (while shortening the time) if someone requests that you do so. Remember, you're making up for all the spontaneous, small interactions that naturally happen when we physically work together. Remember to continue to help others identify and access their strengths during this time. While they may never have been through this perfect storm of change and disruption, they've successfully navigated other challenges in their life. Remind them to use those experiences and tools.
- **Identify Coachable Moments.** If there's a coachable moment (depending on the relationship you have with this person), you can call out the opportunity for coaching by saying, "Would you like to have some coaching on this?" or "Would you like some help figuring this issue out?"

Above all, keep learning and leverage the experience of others who are skilled on different platforms. Finally, be sure to use the full array of coaching skills and processes so that the person you're coaching can clearly see ways they can improve or succeed.

Take Care of Yourself!

Virtual coaching can be intense. The emotions we feel can permeate our interactions. The two-dimensional interaction of virtual coaching can suck our energy as our brains struggle to stay focused without the spark of an in-person meeting. Be sure to take breaks. Allow enough time between meetings (fifteen to thirty minutes) to reflect, walk around, and provide for your needs. Breaks help you stay present and not burn out from the focused interaction. This is true whether you're an introvert or extrovert. In this new environment, introverts may be more comfortable with having a few interactions, and extroverts may seek out interactions more frequently to manage energy. Know your needs and respect them.

Coaching others through change over which we have little or no direct control helps leaders connect with their team's experience. Once that trust and sense of "we're in this together" is created, your team is more likely to engage in what they can influence and control. Individuals are more likely to accept what they do and don't have control over and focus on what's truly possible. Then they can unleash their collective geniuses to pivot and grow in new ways. That's what a coach approach is all about.

NEXT

- Identify your next conversation about change or recognize when you're in the middle of a conversation about change. What best practice described in this chapter will you use?
- Use the coach approach to explore the person or team's reaction to change and stress; be curious, be nonjudgmental, and explore the range of feelings and perceptions about the change.
- Identify the desired outcome (over which those you're coaching have control) and take them through a coaching conversation.
- Identify action steps, however preliminary, that you and they will take next.

16

COACHING DIFFERENCES

*"Conversations and communication are about building something
with another person, and in that building, wrong turns happen.
People think being wrong is the problem rather than
being defensive about what they're wrong about."*

—*Claudia Rankine*

ONCE I'D FINISHED writing most of the chapters in this book, I
met with an African American friend and colleague who'd attended my
professional coaching program. We chatted about our lives and the book's
progress. In addition to coaching and organizational development, both
of us had worked extensively in the areas of diversity and intercultural
communication.

"Jan," she asked, "how have you addressed diversity in your book?"

"I haven't, directly," I confessed. "It feels like too much to do well."

She was surprised, and then she challenged me to find a way. I went back to my hotel room and began to work on this chapter.

The coaching profession has been remiss in addressing bias, race, gender, ethnicity, culture, and other significant differences that affect coaching. It's a blind spot that I hope the international coaching community will continue to illuminate. Increasingly, working with and valuing differences is essential for your success as a leader and the success of your business. When you seek the best team members and include everyone in the candidate pool, you win. When you recognize that there are new and different customer and client possibilities, you win. It's, in short, a competitive advantage across the world.[46]

This business case for inclusion and diversity recognizes that you find the best by seeking those who may show up differently in your workplace. It also means creating an inclusive, respectful workplace where everyone flourishes by bringing their whole selves to work, and not having to check a part of themselves at the door. It means recognizing that when our workplaces reflect the diversity of our current and future customers and clients, we understand and serve others better. In a diverse workplace, innovation's built in. After all, according to Gardenswartz and Rowe in their esteemed book, *The Global Diversity Desk Reference*, "If everybody in the room is the same, you'll have a lot fewer arguments and a lot worse answers."[47] My intention in this chapter is to raise your awareness about how differences can affect your coaching and offer strategies to learn more.

To coach is to be on a journey of learning about ourselves and others. As a leader who coaches, learning about how differences in gender, generation, ethnicity, and economic status impact communication, perspectives, and values is a vital part of that journey. During the years just before and during the pandemic, our culture experienced a collective awakening of what civility means in our world. Not because of our civil rights laws, but because we're realizing how much difference and civility matter. They matter to our society, which is struggling to understand how different lived experiences define our perspectives and impact our future. They matter to our businesses and organizations, which are discovering that diverse teams tend to inspire innovation and create better results. Finally, they matter to our team members, who aspire to learn, develop, and reach their goals. They also need to matter to you as a leader who coaches.

I think of all the ways we differ as layers of diversity.[48] Despite our tendency to focus on only one difference, it's more accurate to understand that we're all made up of layers of cultural influences that create our filters and shape the stories we tell ourselves. While we begin with some personality tendencies when we're born, it's what we learn from all of our cultural influences, e.g., country of origin, sexual orientation, language, race, gender, ethnicity, families, economic status, religion, profession, etc., that shape our behaviors and our values. Some of these differences impact the way we understand and relate to one another—other differences, not so much.

The questions our differences pose to our coaching can be complex. Can you coach people who are visibly—or perhaps invisibly (not apparent from how they appear)—very different from you? Can you understand their challenges and empathize with barriers about which you know little? Yes, you can, and you must because you lead every person. Learning about diversity is a lifelong journey, and there's no shortcut. Like any knowledge you've pursued, you can decide to learn and experience cultures and perspectives that are different than your own. Being in the workplace exposes us to differences if we choose to learn about others. While there aren't any shortcuts to learning about the diversity represented in your workplace and community, here are a few practices to expand your awareness and better coach others.

- **Expose yourself to differences; be curious and open.** Seeking out cultural events and consuming diverse media where the protagonists are non-white, for example, can help you learn about other people's perspectives. There are many documentaries about the lives and perspectives of significant contributors to our culture who are outside the cultural majority. Read literary novels. The psychologist Steven Pinker, in his book *The Better Angels of Our Nature: Why Violence Has Declined,* attributes the rise of the literary novel in the nineteenth century as a force that helped human beings empathize with others who were different. Over time, literary novels (as opposed to pulp fiction) have helped human beings think about themselves from the perspective of others. For example, the pre-Civil War novel *Uncle Tom's Cabin* couldn't have ended slavery. According to many, however, it contributed to its end by enlarging conversations and asking people to put themselves in the position of others. "It's possible that while understanding stories, we have to understand characters, their motivations, interactions, reactions, and goals. We can then improve our ability to understand real people in the real world."[49] Our global workplace demands that we discover how cultures influence everything from communication style and values to what we expect from our leaders. Be aware and commit to discovering what it might mean.

When I first moved to Idaho, I volunteered for the board of the Idaho Black History Museum. I quickly discovered that being Black in Idaho was similar to and different from other contexts where I grew up, such as the military or the East Coast. I realized that even within an ethnicity, there are significantly different perspectives.

- **Be honest with yourself and others about differences.** While it's helpful to connect your experience, however tenuous, with someone who's telling you their story, be clear with yourself and with them that you've never had that experience and that you're willing to learn from them.
- **Avoid acting on assumptions before you've taken the time to validate them.** Be extra vigilant about making unvalidated assumptions about others. Yes, explore and listen to what they're saying. If you don't quite get it, admit it and ask clarifying questions. For example, "I've never had the experience of being

ignored because of how I looked while others are being served. I'd be infuriated. I'm wondering what the impact on you is."

- **Use the language of the other.** When working with others who are visibly different from you or focused on talking about being an outsider or treated as an *other* for whatever reason, use **their** words and metaphors. Then imagine how they might see the issue and work hard to support their voice.

- **Extend your effort to empathize.** It can be challenging to demonstrate empathy when you feel very different than someone. Believe that you can understand and even empathize. Once you believe you can, according to recent research, you can extend an empathic effort—asking questions and listening longer to responses.[50]

- **Find similarities.** Don't just focus on differences; focus on similarities too. Having had the opportunity to travel in and outside of the US has taught me that we have far more similarities with one another; we just need to have the time, patience, and desire to discover them. When you build on similarities, you create more understanding as well as the pathway for building relationships. Identifying similarities can help people feel positive about one another, as if you and they belong to the same group. You encourage that most human of experiences: connection. "I, too, traveled to those countries. It helped me realize how small my world had been. It sounds like that was your experience as well."

- **Build psychological safety.** Inherent in the coaching process is building trust. As a leader who coaches, you've adopted a growth mindset that encourages others to learn and value different perspectives and experiences. When you use the coach approach as a leader, you also communicate that it's okay to make a mistake. You're willing to be vulnerable and share your mistakes and failures when relevant. You make it safe for others to try again and improve.

- **Acknowledge when people feel marginalized.** When a culture marginalizes groups of people, they treat them as if they're insignificant and don't have equal value. You may never have felt that way, but it's important to understand that others have—and for good reason. Or if you have, help others understand what it means if it's important to you. Recognition and understanding go a long way to acknowledging the reality of someone's lived experience. Coaching then supports everyone to decide how they can build on or transcend that experience.

As you lead and coach others who differ from you, realize that if we're open to it, we're learning about one another all the time. I hope the practices in this chapter will help you reach out to understand the perspectives and challenges others experience. The quote by the African American poet, playwright, and essayist Claudia Rankine that begins this chapter points out that there are bound to be wrong turns when we engage in authentic conversations, such as coaching. It's okay not to know and to be wrong when working with others. Commit to learning, accepting, and discovering with others our diverse human experiences.

NEXT

- In your next 1-2-1 meetings with your team members, make time to get to know some of their layers of diversity. Share your own.
- During a coachable moment, listen actively to a perspective you may not understand. Be curious about what it means to the person sharing it.
- What movie, documentary, or novel are you willing to watch or read to learn more about others' lived experiences? What interests you?
- Encourage others from different cultural backgrounds to share their traditions (food, holidays, etc.) and the story behind them with your work team.
- Acknowledge how different influences and backgrounds have helped your organization be more innovative and successful. Seek any programs or training your organization has on inclusion and diversity.

17

HOW COACHING CAN CREATE YOUR BEST CULTURE

"Culture eats strategy for lunch."

—Peter Drucker

PETER DRUCKER'S QUOTE has become a rallying cry for leaders who recognize that unless they create an environment where everyone thrives, the organization will ultimately fail to thrive. People and their motivations, aspirations, and skills make the difference. Culture is complex and elusive. Whether you're a small entrepreneurial organization or a large company, instilling consistent, inspiring, unwritten rules, values, and behaviors in your organization is a priority.

Creating a coaching culture can help. Leaders who coach have discovered that when they spread coaching skills, mindset, and values throughout their organization, coaching becomes a key part of the company's identity. The Center for Creative Leadership puts it this way: "A coaching culture enables radical organizational transformation by building conversational and coaching skills on a daily basis."[51] Ultimately, creating a coaching culture transforms the way leaders and teams interact with one another and their stakeholders. In this chapter, we provide a close-up of the different paths leaders and organizations have chosen to establish a coaching culture and the results that followed.

Leaders saw the possibility of using coaching to help build their culture before I did. From the beginning of developing leaders as coaches, I had doubts. Would leaders see coaching as a powerful way to elevate others? Would they be motivated to practice it and make it part of their leadership? How would leaders from dramatically different industries respond to adopting a coaching mindset? Finally, would organizations invest in developing the capacity to coach in their leaders? I didn't know. But I felt the time was right for all the reasons I've explored in this book. I was surprised when the first organization to take the plunge into creating a coaching culture was a large fire department.

The deputy chief firefighter attended our first program and immediately sponsored a program for his command staff. He saw the potential for his leaders to stop telling others how to solve problems and start coaching them to use their strengths and experiences to create solutions and make decisions. While the chain of command leadership mode is appropriate when fighting a fire, firefighters and their leaders spend most of their time training, developing, preventing fires, implementing policy, educating the community, and creating effective teams at their stations. Those situations require different leadership styles.

Everyone on the command staff learned to coach and was expected to coach others. The word in the department was that when you walked into a command staff's office, you'd be blue-cubed—leaders would consult a small, three-dimensional coaching aid to remind them of the coaching skills and roadmap. Firefighters knew that they no longer could just ask for the answer; they were expected to engage in discovering solutions and choosing how to move forward toward their goals. As a result, leaders weren't burdened with being the center of all knowledge and the only decision-makers. Leaders were now developing and entrusting their teams to use their knowledge to solve issues and perform well. As a result, the leadership pipeline was being filled, confidence in abilities was increasing, and conversations were more collaborative.

That was 2012, and it was the first time we knew that Leaders Who Coach could transform an organization. We knew that a coaching culture isn't an end itself but rather a means to an end. When organizations value and invest in coaching, they imbed the coaching mindset and skills. They create a culture that engages, empowers, and encourages development at all levels. Since then, many businesses, large nonprofit organizations, large departments, and other organizations have intentionally adopted coaching as a leadership competency. While many were unaware of the growing research about the power of coaching cultures, leaders felt the impact of coaching on themselves, and they saw their cultures change.

A small nonprofit that served a large group of stakeholders began their coaching journey slowly, first providing coaching development for their Vice President of Engagement. Next, they extended coaching development opportunities to their entire leadership staff during a two-year period. Everyone who had completed the fourteen-hour program met regularly to practice and discuss their challenges. The coach approach to developing others became an integral part of their culture. Their employee engagement survey scores rose, and some leaders took advantage of advanced coaching skills programs.

In the financial department of a large university, every level of leader attended our coaching program. The common values and skills inherent in coaching helped them build an environment where people felt psychologically safe to speak up about things they wanted to change. The leaders noticed that conflicts were more easily managed because peers listened first. Finally, in an industry where there are plenty of opportunities to go elsewhere, they realized better rates of retention with their valued professionals.

These stories illustrate what studies over the last decade have been reporting. When organizations embrace a coaching culture, they have *higher employee engagement and increased revenues than their industry peers.* Michael Bush, CEO of Best Places to Work, reported in 2020 that across the world, when people are anxious or feel unsupported, they're less likely to interact with others or take healthy risks.[52] Furthermore, when people feel that leaders care about what others think and feel, they're more likely to feel a sense of belonging, which in turn increases productivity and results in higher retention. The benefits of leaders who coach translate into these well-known indicators of workplace engagement.

In addition, the impact of high-potential employees with access to coaching is that those employees are most likely to stay engaged and be productive at work. They're more likely to stay in their organizations and feel that they're making progress toward accomplishing their goals. Coaching and developing your team is even more imperative during the Great Resignation, when turnover and sparse applicants have created strain and pain. Studies in the neuroscience of coaching suggest that peer coaching and leader-to-direct-report coaching might be the only method to bring the benefits of coaching to large numbers of people and change organizational norms and culture.[53] What organization doesn't want those kinds of results? What will it take for your organization to get there?

During the first decade of our coaching program, I worked with more than a dozen small- to medium-sized organizations that were seeking ways to embed coaching into their culture but had limited resources. Their organizational values were consistent with coaching, and they identified a direct connection between coaching and achieving the results they want. In my collaboration with them, my team and I learned that there are potentially five stages that help build coaching cultures successfully over time:

1. Assess how coaching fits for your organization.
2. Form a design team.
3. Develop leaders to use the coaching model.
4. Embed coaching in your organization and keep learning.
5. Provide internal and external coaching experiences.

Stage 1: Assess How Coaching Fits for Your Organization

Do your mission and core values support a unified coaching strategy? Do you believe that developing and empowering your team is the key to delivering results? Is collaboration and leveraging strengths important in how you work with your clients or deliver your service?

Healthwise was the first organization to commit to developing a coaching culture through Leaders Who Coach. Seventy leaders attended our program, and Healthwise supported practice sessions and advanced training. Their established values include collaborating inside and outside the organization, innovation, and responsiveness to the educational needs of a changing healthcare industry. Their culture has been honored as one of the Best Places to Work. Most notably, they report that coaching helped their leaders instill a culture of listening, collaboration, and employee-centered development.

While you might value coaching as a skill, in order to create a coaching culture, you have to assess whether it's important to you and whether it's sufficiently aligned with your core values. If you're willing to invest in making coaching a core competency for leaders, consider these key questions:

- **Does your leadership value a growth mindset?** Growth mindset leaders believe that when people elicit feedback, learn from their mistakes, value effort over talent, and root for each other's success, it fosters success for everyone. They prioritize learning and growing people and teams.

157

- **Do you embrace the expectation that an important role of your leaders is to empower and develop others and generate future leaders?** When your leaders coach, they foster a culture of learning and development in service of the individual, team, and organizational performance. Coaching and developing others (44 percent), engaging and inspiring others (41 percent), and possessing emotional intelligence (35 percent) are *the most valuable skills and competencies for first-time people managers.*[54] Coaching increases a leader's capabilities in all of these areas.

In our experience, leaders at the top make the commitment to a coaching culture after they've personally experienced our program or been professionally coached. It isn't theoretical to them; they understand the power of coaching and how it can create the culture they want.

Stage 2: Form a Design Team

Once you've made the decision to create the capacity for leaders to coach, the next step is to decide how you want to implement it. We've discovered that every organization is different and, as a result, should consider the best ways to bring coaching to their culture.

A design team helps guide the organization through the process. Design teams are made up of influential leaders who are committed to development. The team may include leaders from training, HR, operations, and other high-level leaders. We've learned that working with an internal coaching design team that understands the organization's culture, history, and values is invaluable to a successful coaching culture transformation. Here's how a design team can work:

- The design team reaffirms how coaching is defined and why they believe it will contribute to the organization's success. Consultants meet with the team on a regular basis to further their knowledge and facilitate discussions.

- Design teams choose how to roll out the coaching programs and the ways to communicate the initiatives. The team links coaching to other values and changes in the organization and serves as a steering committee.
- Design teams help consultants/coach facilitators to understand the organization's distinct culture, and they tailor examples and role-plays. The team advises the organization throughout the initiative via webinars and other strategies for sustaining the change.
- Design teams are also essential for creating a coaching infrastructure where the coaching community is supported and rewarded. The team decides how coaching links to people strategies, including talent, leadership, and team development.
- Design teams lead the effort to help coaching become a leadership competency that's continuously developed and measured.

Design teams are an essential step in creating a coaching culture because they help the organization own and implement the change. While closely aligned with the senior leadership team, the team's passion and focus on the coaching culture are key to creating the culture.

Stage 3: Develop Leaders to Become Coaches

Nothing begins a cultural shift more than senior leaders modeling their commitment to learn and implement coaching. The impact can begin with these steps:

- First, the top leadership team attends an intense two-day or fourteen-hour virtual coaching program taught by International Coaching Federation Certified Professional Coaches. This first step helps to create a shared commitment and understanding of the value of coaching in the organization.
- Next, the company carefully chooses leaders for the next program. The design team of one of our clients interviewed attendees extensively, searching for those who would champion the culture

change and were willing to be vulnerable as they role-modeled the new skills. The interviews created a buzz within the organization and a desire to learn these skills.

- The leaders create the space to practice and keep learning. Provide time and structure between each program to strengthen coaching skills in those who initially participated so they can support the next group.

Our *Leaders Who Coach: Essentials* program begins the coaching culture process with either a two-day, highly experiential learning program or a six-module live webinar, with a follow-through webinar one month later (see Appendix C). Recently, our approach was resoundingly supported by research. The August 2018 *Harvard Business Review* article "Most Managers Don't Know How to Coach People, But They Can Learn" reports that the "telling, consulting and micromanaging-as-coaching mentality" used by most managers can be significantly shifted to an evidence-based coaching skill set through a two-day coaching program, with feedback by professional, credentialed coaches.[55]

Due to the challenges of the pandemic, we now have a live online webinar series consisting of six modules over three half-days. The capabilities of Zoom and other platforms allow us to conduct breakout practice sessions (with feedback from coach/facilitators), small group interactions to discuss and brainstorm, and short videos that model coaching. The advantage of this online program is that participants can join us virtually and, like our in-person program, practice coaching in breakout dyads with feedback from the coach/facilitators. The coach/facilitators also provide the participants with mentoring. Both programs include a follow-up webinar one month later to check in on progress and provide additional training. To support continuous coach development, we offer advanced webinars and group mentors to coach sessions.

We've rejected requests to provide our initial *Leaders Who Coach: Essentials* program in a one-day format. Our experience and the research cited above reveal that, on average, learning that's not experiential, including practice, typically results in participants taking away only 10 to 15 percent of the content and probably a lower percentage of the skills. Furthermore, when leaders return to their familiar environment, it's easy to return to the style they previously used. While one-day programs may expose leaders to new concepts and a few skills, those programs cannot provide leaders with the experience to practice and then implement key skills immediately when they return to work. In particular, when leaders have practiced coaching and being coached by others repeatedly, they're more likely to return to their organization ready to coach.

Stage 4: Embed Coaching in Your Organization

Training and coaching leaders is only the beginning of helping you create the culture you want. The following strategies have helped organizations embed the coach approach skills so they're daily, common practices.

- Provide opportunities for leaders to practice their coaching skills. We promote the use of triads in our programs when leaders first learn the coaching skills. Triads consist of the coach, the person being coached, and the person observing coaching behaviors and providing feedback. Give everyone the opportunity to switch roles. Leaders can practice their skills with others they trust, see how others coach, and elicit feedback on what's going well and what they can improve. We also encourage the use of coaching skills in meetings. Finally, we deepen leaders' coaching skills through advanced webinars, internal meetings, and advanced training with leaders.
- Share examples and stories of best practices throughout the organization. These stories might feature customers, vendors, and members of the public, depending on the industry. You can share these stories at your meetings as a regular highlight and also through newsletters and communications from your CEO.

- Integrate coaching values and a growth mindset into the values and best practices you communicate when you onboard new team members and leaders.
- Always connect coaching with your business strategy, purpose, and mission.

These strategies also echo successful change practices. Coaching activities (e.g., 1-2-1 coaching, team coaching, and workgroup coaching with a professional coach practitioner) are rated as the most helpful in achieving the goal of change management initiatives. Using coaching to lead an agile culture means cultivating greater confidence in employees' capabilities in planning and executing change.[56]

Stage 5: Provide Internal and External Coaching Experiences

Another strategy that supports coaching in your culture is to offer the following additional opportunities to be coached:

- Engage external professional coaches for your executives. Our program champions using real situations in which leaders can practice—because when we're coached, the effectiveness and magic of coaching become clear. When leaders seek professional coaching, they also model the value of continuous learning, they receive feedback, and they're challenged to grow in ways they may rarely experience inside their organization.
- Consider establishing a team of internal coaches. One of our clients also invested in advanced coaching training for a small group of individuals who might provide short-term coaching to those who don't report to them. This team of internal coaches provided limited coaching to team members outside their departments. We helped them navigate the boundaries as well as the ethical and power dynamics of internal coaches. We found that these high-performing leader coaches developed advanced

coaching skills, and they provided a low-cost resource for others in the organization. By investing in these internal coaches, the organization offered in-depth growth opportunities for individuals and created a resource for their entire organization.

- Encourage peer-to-peer coaching. When peers coach one another, they feel more connected and supported. The *Harvard Business Review* article "How Peer Coaching Can Make Work Less Lonely" reports, "Peer coaching is about cultivating a network of allies that can provide mutual support in creating positive change to improve performance and addresses the roots of loneliness at work."[57] Whether at work or at home, loneliness can deepen stress and provide the impetus for the best employees to seek positions elsewhere. Next to the relationship with our direct manager, the extent we feel connected to our work peers is an important predictor of retention and performance.

The impact of creating a coaching culture to help leaders live their values and reach their goals is still being measured. Here's a client story about why their bilingual organization embarked on their coaching culture journey—and what they noticed:

We had a redesign in our agency six years ago. Our priorities were in line, but we still had a residue of our old culture and old habits. We also had untapped talent that wasn't being developed because we were so busy. We made the decision to become a coaching culture to improve communication and develop our teams. When leaders coach, it takes pressure off those leaders to figure everything out. Now instead of just delegating, we coach our staff and teams to come up with their own solutions and make better decisions.

The impact has filtered all the way down to our line staff. As a result, there's been a morale shift. People feel empowered to generate ideas and be creative. They have more confidence in one another to face challenges. It's a culture change. Our communication has improved, it's easier for us to solve issues, and we've built amazing trust between leaders and staff. It's a great feeling to see our teams growing, and they're better off as a result of coaching.

The best investment you can make is developing your employees. If you have well-developed employees, your results are going to follow. Get the right people to lead your coaching culture. You will reap benefits for years to come.

What can get in the way of creating a coaching culture? In 2014, the International Coaching Federation study entitled *Building a Coaching Culture with Managers and Leaders* asked leaders and organizations to identify what prevents them from using their coaching skills. In addition to time, command-and-control, and the internal impediments described above, the study identified these cultural issues:

- Lack of budget for training
- Poor support for continuing to develop coaching skills
- Lack of integration of coaching into the culture
- Short-term skill development
- Limited support from senior leaders
- Inability to measure impact

In coaching cultures that sustain best practices and results, clients invest their money and time carefully, believing leaders who coach will enable them to accomplish their goals. We work side by side in partnership with clients, and they've shown us that, over time, they can create a coaching culture that helps them retain their best team members and encourage everyone to reach the high goals they've set.

Your journey to a coaching culture may be different. We offer these best practices to encourage you. No matter how small or large, you can do it. To make coaching part of your culture, gather your leaders and make a plan that will best fit your vision and resources.

NEXT

- Gather like-minded leaders to consider how developing coaching could positively benefit your leaders and organization.
- How are you aligned, and how are your perceptions different?
- What are the first (or next) steps you can take to become a coaching culture?

18

LEADER COACHING PRACTICES OF HIGH INTEGRITY: DO GOOD AND DO NO HARM

"Only credible leaders earn commitment, and only commitment builds and regenerates great organizations and communities."

—James M. Kouzes & Barry Z. Posner

WHEN LEADERS COACH, they help teams and team members to develop and grow. The helping value of the conversation is high. This isn't the time to focus on business imperatives such as KPIs and corporate goals. Yes, as we have shared in other chapters, your coaching unquestionably has an impact on your team accomplishing their aspirations and your organizational objectives. However, you wear different leadership hats to achieve results in different ways. When leaders put on their coaching hats, they tell us they anticipate conflicts with their other hats. This chapter provides guidelines to help you stay in the sweet spot of coaching. When you do so with high integrity, it minimizes conflicts and supports your impact.

Be Professional and Respectful

When you use the following best practices, you can be confident that you're on a path that not only won't do any harm but also will greatly benefit others and your organization.

Honor your appointments. Keep your word. If you commit to meeting with someone, do it. Follow through. Be clear about the time you have and what you can do to create more time if that's needed. Create the habit for yourself and model it for others. Life happens, priorities change, and leaders have full plates. Everyone understands that critical things come up occasionally. Honoring appointments is a simple way to show that you care and respect others' time.

Honor confidentiality. In your conversations, be clear at the beginning about whether or not the entire conversation can be confidential. There are times when that isn't possible for leaders. Here's an example:

> Avani was looking forward to her weekly meeting with her direct report, Marsha. Over the last year, trust had been built, and Marsha seemed comfortable bringing up issues that were rich opportunities for coaching. This time, however, Marsha looked distressed. She shared that Mike, a co-worker, had been sarcastic to her in front of others, raising his voice when critiquing her product and standing too close in an intimidating way when he spoke with her. When she asked him to give her more space, he gave her the silent treatment and wouldn't talk to her for a week. She stated that she wanted help to find a way to respond to Mike's behavior. Marsha was convinced that if she figured out what she did to deserve his behavior and how she could change, Mike would stop.
>
> As Avani listened to Marsha describing Mike's yelling, put-downs, and retaliatory silence, she realized that the problem wasn't Marsha's; it

was hers as a leader in the company. Avani recognized the signs of possible bullying and gender harassment and knew she had a responsibility to report the behavior for possible investigation. She also needed to protect Marsha from Mike's behavior while she and the company looked into what was happening.

Avani decided to change the focus of their conversation. She calmly told Marsha that she had an obligation to share the information outside their meeting. Marsha was furious and exclaimed that she was capable of handling the situation and that she expected to be coached, not disempowered. Avani listened carefully and acknowledged how Marsha might have felt betrayed. Then she gently explained the why behind the company's policy regarding harassment. And she was clear and firm about the next steps.

Honor limits. If the topic is outside your competency and must be addressed, bring in the right people or refer the person you're coaching to an expert in that area. Sharing heartfelt emotions is common when leaders are coaching. It's when those emotions are significantly blocking a person from coping or performing that other expertise may be needed. You're not a counselor—you're a leader who coaches. Use the coaching process as a way to help explore other options and fears about reaching out. Provide additional resources, such as an Employee Assistance Program.

At their last weekly 1-2-1 conversation, Eric told his manager, Bill, that his father had gone into hospice care and didn't have long to live. Bill started this week's 1-2-1 by asking Eric about his father. Eric's eyes immediately began to fill with tears, and he acknowledged that he could barely focus on work because of how hard it was to visit his dying father. He had just reconciled with him and regretted not having done so sooner. Eric said he was feeling alone and didn't know what to do with his feelings.

Bill realized very quickly that Eric's grief and conflicted feelings were beyond the scope of a coaching conversation. He acknowledged the depth of Eric's loss and then focused on what Eric needed and what would support and help him.

For the next fifteen minutes, Bill asked a series of questions. "As I hear you talk, it sounds like you've been feeling this way for a couple of weeks now. What kind of help and support do you want? How else have you considered getting help? If you do nothing, what might happen a week or two from now?" He ended with, "What's getting in the way of you getting more help and support?"

Bill also encouraged Eric to consider family leave and shared how he sought help from a counselor when a close friend of his passed away. Finally, Bill mentioned the Employee Assistance Program and other resources available in the company's benefit plan.

Remain objective. Although we seek to be present and turn off our biases, fears, and needs, they sometimes emerge. We're human beings with our own stories and experiences. Our stereotypes regarding gender, ethnicity, backgrounds, etc., can slant our questions and hijack our coaching.

Because the practice of coaching focuses on understanding and helping others and staying away from your advice, it has a built-in objective filter. However, you can't turn off your perceptions entirely. Pay attention to your internal dialogue and notice when you feel judgmental or your emotions are triggered by what the person says. Use active listening skills to refocus and stick with how the person is defining their experiences and wants. Most importantly, use the coaching process to guide the conversation and stay clear of your agenda. Understanding your biases is a lifelong process, and the only way to understand them is to expose yourself to differences, listen carefully to other people's stories, and be open to feedback.

Be honest. Underlying every trusting relationship is a belief that the other person's doing their best to be authentic and real. It's no different in coaching. If you aren't psychologically available to coach, let others know and schedule a time when you are. If you don't understand what someone's saying or what they're feeling, let them know and ask for clarification; don't just play along. If you can deliver helpful, supportive feedback about the way someone's coming across, think about how you can best do this. If something emerges that presents a conflict of interest for you that you can't put aside, let the other person know and figure out an alternative way for them to get their needs met.

Honesty in coaching is critical. Coaching requires a balance between projecting care and remaining separate. As a leader who coaches, you're detached and nonjudgmental, so you can provide a safe place for the person to hear themselves and discover their solutions. You act as a human mirror to reflect what the person's saying, feeling, and wanting through different lenses. On the other hand, it's important to know when it's not the right time for you to wear that hat.

View others as whole and resourceful. At the core of the coach approach is the fundamental belief that others aren't broken. The inspiration for this positive psychology perspective came from Alfred Adler, the father of modern individual psychology. He rejected the focus on sickness in behavior and instead assumed that humans had far-reaching capabilities and resources with which to cope with life. We're not wrong. We routinely marshal our strengths, experiences, and teams to address the many challenges we face. We're the experts when it comes to us. Believe and know that this is true.

When you believe that others are whole and resourceful, you challenge assumptions and probe for possibilities. When you adopt this growth mindset to coaching others, the impact is magical. The person senses your attitude and sees that they're capable and can confidently take the next step. One way to reinforce these beliefs is to check your assumptions about others and reflect on the time you have spent with them. What did you learn about their strengths and capabilities that you didn't know before? What surprised you? I constantly discover how limited my perspectives are and how much depth there is to each person.

Keep Learning and Developing

Marsha Reynolds, a renowned coaching leader and developer of coaches, tells the story of her 8,000-foot climb to Machu Pichu in Peru. Rigorous and sometimes harrowing, she asked her guide if he still considered the climb to be hard. "It's not so bad," the guide responded. "I'm always learning."

As a leader who coaches, you're always learning about others, your organization, and yourself. Whether you're being coached by a professional or a peer, being willing to be vulnerable and ask for help is an essential practice for being a leader who coaches. As trust grows between leaders and their teams, everyone's more open to bringing difficult conversations to you and your coaching conversations. Be ready. Remember to open the door to learning, even when you feel defensive and possibly threatened. Above all, stay in your listening mode.

During a 1-2-1, Amy asked Tyrone one of her routine coaching questions. "Hey, Tyrone, what's next for you as you look ahead in your career?"

Tyrone stopped, looked at her intently, and said, "Well, I think I'll have to leave to pursue my dream of becoming an entrepreneur."

Amy was floored. Tyrone was a highly valued technical lead, and she was counting on him to manage the next product launch. Her first reaction was to ask why and try to talk him out of it. But she stopped herself just in time and asked, "So, can you tell me more about what that looks like for you?"

Put On Your Coaching Hat and Practice

What could be more obvious? We simply don't get better at anything by thinking about it. Practice coaching every day by using specific skills such as coaching questions, encouraging, and active listening. Create formal coachable moments and request that others use their 1-2-1s for coaching. Use coaching with your kids (especially teenagers). Employ coaching skills in group settings with your team or at board meetings. Seek out coachable moments. Notice how and when you shift in and out of coaching. Eventually, coaching will become part of you, and although the skills and process are universally effective, your style will emerge.

When Gunther returned from the coaching program, his colleagues noticed an immediate change. He used to be all fired up to tell people what to do. Now he spends more time listening and helping his team get to the heart of the matter by coaching. His relationships with others have changed. Coaching has become part of his "leadership brand." His team expects him to coach when appropriate.

Nothing sends a louder message than what you *do*. If your actions and words don't match, your lack of integrity will impact your credibility as a leader. Remember, when you coach, you're also deciding the kind of leader you want to be and the kind of culture you want to build. Practice your coaching and build your vision.

NEXT

1. Which of these coaching practices are clear and natural for you?

   - Being respectful and professional
   - Honoring limits
   - Remaining objective
   - Being honest
   - Viewing others as whole and resourceful
   - Continually learning and developing
   - Practicing your coaching

2. Which ones may be more challenging?
3. Note one way you'll intentionally live these ethical practices.
4. What opportunities exist for you to be coached (by your peers, etc.)?

19

COACH ME TO COACH

"Grounded confidence is the messy process of learning and unlearning, practicing and failing, and surviving a few misses."

—Brené Brown

EVERY COACHING CONVERSATION ends with what's next. It ends with a new beginning. What are your next steps to becoming a leader who coaches? Begin by painting a picture of the leader you want to be and articulating your purpose as a leader who coaches. You begin by taking the next steps to reach your destination—becoming a leader who coaches. Use the PASN Roadmap to coach yourself and create a plan for your next steps.

When I met Angelina, she was a seasoned nursing leader. She shared that what led her to seek out coach training was the feedback she received from others. People often described her style of leading as a coaching style. She wasn't sure what that meant, so she researched coaching and sought out a coaching program to take her natural style to the next level. With support, she took a leave from leading and applied her coaching to other leaders in a large healthcare business. She practiced, sought out coach mentoring, and honed her coach leadership style. Finally, it was time to return to a challenging leadership role: leading a large leadership team of nurses.

Angelina describes the impact of her coaching skills as profound. To her core, she believes that the solutions are found with her team and their teams. The primary purpose of her leadership is to help others figure out the core issues, coach them to discover solutions, and make a plan to move forward.

For example, one of her managers wasn't following through on goals—she complained that her team didn't have enough resources to deal with the challenges of COVID-19. She was stuck in indecision—how could she possibly move forward? Angelina acknowledged that the lack of resources was a real challenge.

She asked her manager, "What would you do if you had the resources?" The question created a dialogue about her team's needs, a plan to implement the resources when they showed up, and some immediate strategies to diminish the stress on her team.

Angelina reflected, "The pressure of the everyday grind can lead to blind spots about what's possible. I ask the people I coach to imagine the ideal team or outcome, and that question helps them to explore with one another how they can get there. People are more committed to their solutions because they've designed them. I've also discovered that through my coaching, I can grow the next leaders to lead when I step away." Angelina reports that 50 to 70 percent of her time is spent coaching individuals and her team. Her purpose in being a leader who coaches is to develop everyone around her.

What's your purpose in being a leader who coaches? I invite you to use the following steps to form a thirty-day plan to become a leader who coaches. See Appendix C for a *Coach Me Worksheet.*

Your Thirty-Day Coach Plan

1. Purpose—*Define Your Purpose as a Leader*

Every coaching journey starts with what you want, where you're going, and what's important to you. What is your overall purpose as a leader? Don't bother to wordsmith—just write down the first sentences that come to your mind.

Jackson was overwhelmed with how often his team interrupted him with problems and needs. He was neglecting his leadership projects for the company, but he didn't want to reject his team's requests for his help. Jackson had always seen his leadership purpose as serving others to grow them and the business. Ironically, he realized that he was so busy helping others that he wasn't helping them grow. Coaching, he decided, would support his leadership purpose.

What's the *why* of your leadership? Make it personal. How can coaching serve your why? How is coaching integral to achieving that purpose?

2. Ascertain—Take a Coaching Skills Self-Audit

Think about the ideas, skills, beliefs, mindset, and other coaching knowledge you now possess. What strengths do you already have that are part of the coach approach? Do you get the concept of an open-ended question that encourages deep exploration? Are you naturally empathetic toward others—can you see the world from their

177

perspective? Are you curious about what others think, feel, and want? To what extent do you approach your role as leader with a growth mindset?

Your Coaching Strengths:

In what areas would you like to improve? Perhaps you're empathetic and don't know how to express that when you listen to others. Or maybe stopping your advice monster is tough for you; restraining that habit can be a good first step. Perhaps remembering to ask open-ended questions during coaching conversations is a struggle. In what other areas would you like to improve? Pick one or two skills that would make a difference right now. If you were to improve those skills, what would be the outcome? What would be the impact on others if you did so?

One (or Two) Coach Areas to Improve

Jackson's first thirty-day goal was expressed as: coach instead of tell. He realized telling and expertise had been his default mode as a leader, based on his past role models. For him, that transitioned into asking open-ended coaching questions and actively listening first when people came to his office. He decided to act on the belief that his team had the answers. Jackson also committed to putting aside his own solutions so he could focus on their ideas.

3. Strategize the Way

As you coach yourself to create an effective thirty-day plan to improve your coaching skills as a leader, generate specific ideas about when and with whom you could practice coaching and how you might measure your improvement each week.

When Jackson asked himself what steps he could take every day to accomplish his plan to practice two coaching skills—questioning and listening—he had to think hard about possible coachable moments. "When someone comes into my office, I'm first going to ask them what they want out of the conversation. I'm not going to assume that I know. Then I'll be curious and say something like, 'Tell me what led to this situation and what you've done thus far.' I think I could practice that sequence at least once a day."

That was Jackson's first two-week plan. His second two-week plan was to communicate his belief in his team's abilities and skills as a way of letting them know they had the resources to help solve the problem. What could he say? "I could ask them about their peak performance experience and encourage them to use their strengths in the situation they're presenting. I can do that at least once a week, in team meetings as well as individual meetings."

Perhaps your goal is to express empathy. What would that sound like? How can you listen actively and use feeling words to describe what you're hearing? When and with whom would you like to practice being more empathetic—and what's an easy first step? What are the possible coaching moments with someone you know and trust? What exactly do you want to do differently?

List specific ways you'd like to improve your identified coaching skill/approach:

With whom would you like to practice?

What are the coachable moments?

4. Next—Identify Obstacles and Create Action Steps

Accountability is one of the hallmarks of coaching success. How do you shape realistic expectations for yourself *and* seek out support from others to accomplish your goal? Creating clear action steps is critical to being accountable in coaching, so you can assess your progress, learn from your mistakes, and build the confidence to stretch further. Involving others in your journey can help keep you on track; asking for support and encouragement builds confidence. Take the ideas listed in your strategy list and define three specific action steps.

No coaching plan is complete unless you understand the potential obstacles. These may be internal obstacles such as habits, beliefs, and making time. Or they may be external, such as the expectations or demands of others. Naming the obstacles will help you anticipate and plan to overcome them.

Think carefully about these questions as you continue to define your path. You may come back to these questions multiple times to flesh out what will help you clear the path.

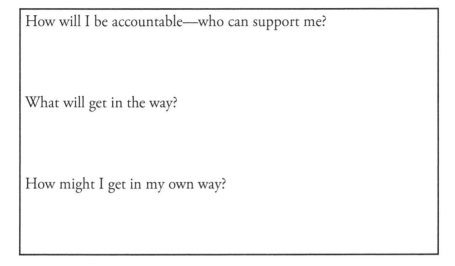

How will I be accountable—who can support me?

What will get in the way?

How might I get in my own way?

Jackson knew that the first two weeks of coaching would be challenging, and he wanted to continue to get better. His action step for the third and fourth week was to practice the PASN Roadmap with at least three team members. He expressed it this way: "It's hard to help people focus, and yet if I don't, how can they make progress? My ultimate goal for both individual and team meetings is to help them focus with good questions and listen to flesh out the core issue or question." Strategizing was a strength for Jackson, but he wanted to encourage others to offer their ideas and solutions. Finally, he wanted to end his conversations by challenging others to define an action plan.

Jackson's NEXT thirty-day plan was good, although it was more challenging than he imagined. One obstacle, he realized, was his habits. Just stopping the advice monster and telling was challenging. Substituting the new behaviors of listening and asking questions took a lot of bandwidth in his mind. It was a big change. So he decided to stick with his first week's goal for three weeks before implementing the entire coaching roadmap. "I realized that my brain's wiring had to change, and it would only change if I kept practicing a few skills every day."

Jackson took one more step—he asked his boss to support his enrolling in a leader-based coaching program. He realized that without more practice, feedback, and knowledge, it would be tough to fully develop his coaching skills.

Coaching yourself to coach can help you begin your journey to becoming a leader who coaches or deepen your coaching skills if you're already on that path. It only takes a few minutes to write down your intentions, identify how you want to change, and begin to practice coaching.

NEXT

Follow through with one strategy, one skill, or one insight you gained from reading this book. Notice what happens to you and to others.

- Follow through with hiring a professional coach to help you develop your leadership and your awareness of the coaching process.
- Follow through by supporting others in your organization to learn to coach.

APPENDIX A:
KEY COACHING SKILLS

The three coaching skills of listening actively, asking powerful questions, and encouraging are essential for every part of the PASN Roadmap. To help you effectively focus your skills, I offer this guide. Review these techniques before you coach, then write them down or copy them to display when you're on your Zoom meetings. Pick ones that feel somewhat natural, and try new ones when you're ready. Always remember that coaching is learned by practicing, reflecting, and redoing.

Listen Actively

Techniques can help us shape our responses to keep the focus on the person we're coaching and understand the meaning of their communication. As long as your intent and mindset are clear, these techniques won't sound robotic to the person you're coaching. Here are a few phrases to keep in mind as you actively listen to others:

- I'm hearing you say . . .
- You seem to be saying/feeling . . .
- It sounds like . . .
- If I'm understanding you correctly, you think/feel . . .
- I sense that . . .
- It appears to me . . .
- What I'm hearing/perceiving/experiencing . . .
- As I hear you talk, I'm noticing . . .
- You want to . . .

Ask Powerful Coaching Questions

Coaching questions are the most powerful when they're used in the stage of the PASN Roadmap that you and the person are in. These questions (and many more) specifically address the focus of that stage of the roadmap. Remember that listening and encouraging are always present in a coaching conversation.

PASN Roadmap

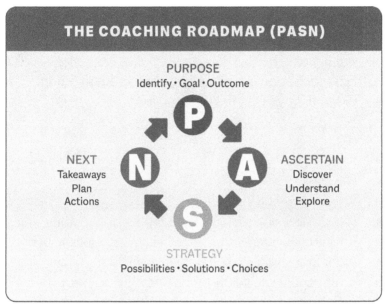

© 2021 Jan Salisbury

P—Purpose
- How can I help?
- What would you like to walk out of here with today?
- What outcome would you like from our time today?

A—Ascertain
- How important is that to you?
- What does that (success, fear, etc.) look like and feel like?
- What's the impact of ____on you/others/the business?
- Can you share an example of what you mean?
- What's your contribution to this situation?
- How do others around you see this situation?
- What are the long-term implications if this situation doesn't change?

S—Strategizing

- If this were successful, what would that look like?
- What's possible here? What else is possible?
- What's missing from your ideas?
- When have you been in this situation before, and what have you done?
- How could you apply your strengths to this situation?
- How might you get in your own way?

N—Next

- Based on our conversation today, what are you taking forward?
- How will you do so?
- When will you do so?
- What's the first step you will take forward to achieving your goal?
- What are the internal and external barriers to following through?
- What may stop you or slow you down?
- What support do you need, and who can support you?
- Can you summarize what you've decided?

Encourage

The act of encouraging takes many forms. Pepper your conversations with authentic recognition or appreciation of anything that says, "You are making progress," or, "You are courageous to take on this challenge." One way is to take time to identify specific strengths that a person can intentionally call on to reach his or her goals.

The following questions are designed to encourage the person and help them identify their strengths:

- Think about the last time you felt joyful and energized at work. What specifically were you doing?
- What do you do in your role that inspires you to do more?
- How would others around you describe your strengths?
- What do you do that you'd like to do more of? Why?

APPENDIX B: THE GOTTMAN FEELING WHEEL

Use this wheel to help you and others develop a language for emotions. They're grouped in similar categories to help you see if different words can express the nuances of how you feel. There's no right or wrong label; get familiar with the wheel by playing with it. Start on the outer wheel and see how it relates to the more basic emotional labels.

The Feeling Wheel

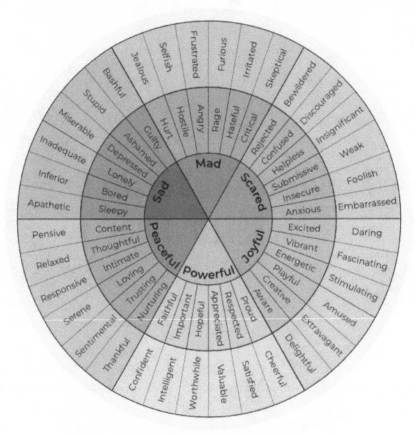

The Gottman Institute
Developed by Dr. Gloria Willcox

APPENDIX C:
YOUR COACH ME PLAN

Use this template to plan your coaching journey. Then revise it as you become clearer and accomplish your steps.

PURPOSE—Define Your Purpose as a Leader

Your Purpose:

ASCERTAIN—Take a Coaching Skills Self-Audit

Your Coaching Strengths:

One or Two Coach Areas to Improve:

STRATEGIZE THE WAY

What are specific ways you'd like to improve your identified coaching skill/approach?

With whom would you like to practice?

What are the coachable moments?

NEXT—Identify Obstacles and Create Action Steps

How will you be accountable—who can support you?

What will get in the way?

How might you get in your own way?

ACKNOWLEDGMENTS

I'm grateful to all the leaders who joined me to become leaders who coach. Thank you for your feedback and for sharing your learning and stories. You wrote this book with me. You continue to inspire me about the power of the coach approach to leading. My Vistage members have supported me throughout this journey, always reminding me that if you want to go fast, go alone, but if you want to go far, go with others.

This book wouldn't exist without the encouragement and input from my colleagues. Thank you Alison Hendren, Founder of Coaching Out of the Box®. Your 5/5/5 coaching model was absolutely essential to the success of *Leaders Who Coach*. I appreciate your support and openness to our *Leaders Who Coach* initiatives.

I am indebted to my co-founder, Dawn Monroe, for your willingness to collaborate with me to create *Leaders Who Coach*. You were all in, and your experience and commitment made the difference.

Thank you to my co-coach/facilitators of *Leaders Who Coach* (Tom Hardison) and especially Paul Terry for your partnership as we created online programs and continue to enrich our program with Advanced Workshops and Mentoring. Without you, Tenora Grigsby, there wouldn't be a chapter on coaching differences. Thank you for challenging me to write it.

To my Vistage colleagues Ron Gambassi, Tammy Adams, and David Spann, I appreciate how you've challenged me to think and be better. Finally, thank you to my coach, Lerae Gidyk, who nurtured my dreams, modeled the way, and challenged me to overcome my doubts.

NOTES

1   John H. Zenger and Kathleen Stinnett, *The Extraordinary Coach: How the Best Leaders Help Others Grow* (New York: McGraw-Hill Education, 2010).

2   Edgar Schein, *Humble Enquiry: The Gentle Art of Asking Instead of Telling* (San Francisco: Berrett-Koehler Publishers, 2013).

3   Alison Hendren, "Bringing Coaching into Healthcare: How 3 Organizations Using 3 Different Approaches Achieved Powerful Results," paper and oral presentation to the *Institute of Coaching*, Harvard Medical School and McClean Hospital, September 2015.

4   Marco Iacoboni, *Mirroring People: The Science of Empathy and How We Connect with Others* (New York: Picador, 2008).

5   Lisa Feldman Barrett, *How Emotions are Made: The Secret Life of the Brain* (Boston: Mariner Books, 2017).

6   Richard E. Boyatzis and Anthony Jack, "The Neuroscience of Coaching," *Consulting Psychology Journal Practice and Research,* 2018.

7   Schein, *Humble Inquiry.*

8   Adam Grant, *Think Again: The Power of Knowing What You Don't Know* (New York: Viking, 2021).

9   The Arbinger Institute, *The Outward Mindset: How to Change Lives and Transform Organizations* (Oakland, CA: Berrett-Koehler Publishers, Inc., 2016, 2019).

10 Carol S. Dweck, PhD, *Mindset: The New Psychology of Success* (New York: Ballantine Books, 2007).

11 See more on this topic in Marshall Goldsmith's *What Got You Here Won't Get You There: How Successful People Become Even More Successful* (London: Profile Books, 2008).

12 Alex "Sandy" Pentland, "The New Science of Building Great Teams," *Harvard Business Review Magazine*, April 19, 2012, https://hbr.org/2012/04/the-new-science-of-building-great-teams.

13 Hendren, "Bringing Coaching into Healthcare."

14 Brené Brown, *Dare to Lead: Brave Work. Tough Conversations. Whole Hearts* (New York: Random House, 2018), 19.

15 Jim Collins, *Good to Great: Why Some Companies Make the Leap . . . and Others Don't* (New York: HarperCollins Publishers, 2001).

16 Goldsmith, *What Got You Here Won't Get You There.*

17 Kenneth Nowack and Paul Zak, "Empathy Enhancing Antidotes for Interpersonally Toxic Leaders," *Consulting Psychology Journal: Practice and Research,* 2020, Vol. 72, No. 2, 119–133.

18 Nowack and Zak, "Empathy Enhancing Antidotes."

19 Nowack and Zak, "Empathy Enhancing Antidotes."

20 Larry Sternberg and Kim Turnage, *Managing to Make a Difference: How to Engage, Retain, and Develop Talent for Maximum Performance* (Hoboken, NJ: John Wiley & Sons, 2017).

21 Sternberg & Turnage, *Managing to Make a Difference.*

22 Elliot T. Berkman, "The Neuroscience of Goals and Behavior Change," *Consulting Psychology Journal: Practice and Research*, 70, no. 1, (2018): 28–44.

23 Marcia Reynolds, *Coach the Person, Not the Problem: A Guide to Using Reflective Inquiry* (San Francisco: Berrett-Koehler, 2020).

24 The PASN Roadmap is explained in detail in Appendix A.

25 Deborah Welch, Karen Grossaint, Katherine Reid, and Cindy Walker, "Strengths-Based Leadership Development: Insights from Expert Coaches," *Consulting Psychology Journal: Practice and Research*, 2014, Vol. 66, No. 1, 20–37.

26 Welch, et.al, "Strengths-Based Leadership Development."

27 VIA Institutes in Character, "Values In Action Character Assessment," https://www.viacharacter.org/account/register.

28 Tablegroup. "The 6 Types of Working Genius," accessed March 3, 2022, https://www.workinggenius.com.

29 Marcus Buckingham and Donald O. Clifton, PhD, *Now, Discover Your Strengths* (New York: The Free Press, 2001).

30 VIA Institute on Character, "The VIA Character Strengths Survey."

31 "IBM Australia Uses the VIA," YouTube Video, 6:25, December 20, 2012, https://www.youtube.com/watch?v=SkofIsqUbD4.

32 Morgan W. McCall, Jr., & Michael M. Lombardo, "Off The Track: Why and How Successful Executives Get Derailed," *Center for Creative Leadership,* Technical Report No. 21, 1983, http://cclinnovation.org/wp-content/uploads/2020/03/off-the-track-why-successful-executives-get-derailed.pdf.

33 Boyatzis and Jack, *The Neuroscience of Coaching.*

34 Daniel J. Siegel, *The Developing Mind: How Relationships and the Brain Interact to Shape Who We Are* (New York: The Guilford Press, 2020).

35 Ken Blanchard and Spencer Johnson, MD, *The New One-Minute Manager (*New York: William Morrow, 2016).

36 "Coaching Out of the Box," 2015.

37 Blessing White, *The "X" Model of Engagement,* YouTube Video, 7:43 minutes, 2012, https://www.youtube.com/watch?v=SQSccH_I47c.

38 Peter Cappelli & Anna Tavis, "The Performance Management Revolution," *Harvard Business School Magazine*, October, 2016.

39 Reldan S. Nadler, PsyD, *Leading with Emotional Intelligence: Hands-On Strategies for Building Confident and Collaborative Star Performers* (New York: McGraw-Hill Press, 2011).

40 Gino Wickman, *Traction: Get a Grip on Your* Business (Dallas, TX: Benbella Books, Inc., 2012).

41 The Arbinger Institute, *The Outward Mindset: Seeing Beyond Ourselves* (San Francisco: Berrett-Koehler, 2016).

42 Viktor E. Frankl, *Man's Search for Meaning* (Boston: Beacon Press, 2006).

43 Susan Scott, *Fierce Conversations: Achieving Success at Work and in Life One Conversation at a Time* (New York: Fierce, Inc., 2017).

44 Richard E. Boyatzis and Anthony Jack, "The Neuroscience of Coaching," *Consulting Psychology Journal Practice and Research,* 70, No. 1, 2018:11–17.

45 Jeffrey Hiatt, *A Model for Change in Business, Government and Our Community* (Fort Collins, CO: Prosci Inc., 2006).

46 Lee Gardenswartz and Anita Rowe, *The Global Diversity Desk Reference* (San Francisco: John Wiley & Sons, 2003).

47 Gardenswartz and Rowe, *The Global Diversity Desk Reference,* p. 74.

48 Lee Gardenswartz and Anita Rowe, *Diverse Teams at Work: Capitalizing on the Power of Diversity* (Alexandria, VA: Society for Human Resource Management, 2003).

49 Ashley Abrahamson, "Cultivating Empathy," *Monitor on Psychology,* November 1, 2021, Vol. 52, No. 8, p. 50.

50 Abrahamson, "Cultivating Empathy."

51 Center for Creative Leadership. https://www.ccl.org/?utm_source=google&utm_medium=cpc&utm_campaign&keyword=center%20for%20creative%20leadership&matchtype=p&gclid=EAIaIQobChMI2NTF_JLn9QIVEg_nCh0yIQl7EAAYASAAEgIrMfD_BwE.

52 Michael Bush, "Best Places to Work Results," PowerPoint presentation, Vistage Chair World, San Diego, 2020.

53 Boyatzis and Jack, "The Neuroscience of Coaching."

54 Bush, "Best Places to Work Results."

55 Julia Milner and Trenton Milner, "Most Managers Don't Know How to Coach People. But They Can Learn," *Harvard Business Review,* August 14, 2018, https://hbr.org/2018/08/most-managers-dont-know-how-to-coach-people-but-they-can-learn.

56 Allen Trivedi, "How To (Really) Build an Agile Culture through Coaching Skills," *Forbes.com,* Feb. 27, 2018, https://www.forbes.com/sites/forbescoachescouncil/2018/02/27/how-to-really-build-an-agile-culture-through-coaching-skills/?sh=7a9f480a1e1e.

57 Norian Caporale-Berkowitz and Stewart D. Friedman, "How Peer Coaching Can Make Work Less Lonely," *Harvard Business Review Daily,* October 12, 2018.

ABOUT THE AUTHOR

Jan Salisbury, MS MCC, is the president of Salisbury Consulting and a founding partner of Leaders Who Coach LLC. Since 2014, she's served as the chair of Vistage Peer Advisory CEO and Key Executive Boards and is a Master Certified Executive Coach with the International Coaching Federation (ICF). As the President of Salisbury Consulting and Leaders Who Coach, Jan's businesses are committed to developing leaders at all levels, leaders who in turn generate cultures and teams where everyone thrives. She also mentors coaches for professional ICF certification. Early in her career, Jan taught psychology at the undergraduate and graduate levels and has also presented programs in areas such as coaching, leadership, emotional intelligence, diversity, and creating a respectful workplace to her business and non-profit clients and to professional organizations, including the ICF Coaching Chapters, the American Bar Association, and the American

Psychological Association. She's co-authored articles in professional journals as well as the book *Investigating Harassment and Discrimination Complaints*. She's a co-founder and former President of the High County IFC Coaching Chapter that includes Idaho, Montana, Utah, Wyoming, North and South Dakota. Jan spends her free time exploring different cultures, playing on rivers, skiing, and bicycling with her husband, John.

ABOUT LEADERS WHO COACH, LLC

Leaders Who Coach, LLC (LWC) was founded in 2010 and has served more than ninety organizations and seven hundred leaders. We rely on proven techniques for developing talent strategies using the most advanced coaching skills. Our company's successful track record includes coaching work with a diverse range of clients, from international organizations to entrepreneurs. LWC develops customized coaching programs designed specifically for each client in industries such as technology, legal, manufacturing, not-for-profit, higher education, government, and public utilities. These are just a few examples of industries that have used executive coaching to improve team performance and development.

As an International Coaching Federation (ICF) Master Certified Coach, coaching facilitator Jan Salisbury and her team have developed a system of coaching programs in conjunction with a tailor-made approach to executive coaching. This unique approach builds a growth mindset with a coaching culture that increases performance and develops the potential of individuals, teams, leaders, and the organization as a whole.

Unlike similar programs, the LWC team isn't satisfied with simply transferring our extensive knowledge and proven methods to our clients. We have a passion for creating a blueprint for every client that provides a clear path to create a coaching culture and a more productive organization. Our goal is to change an entire organization's way of thinking for real transformation. The LWC team works side by side with their clients as they build their coaching skills, empower their teams, and ultimately imbed a coaching culture that becomes a part of daily work life.

The LWC leadership coaching skills journey often begins with the *Leaders Who Coach: Essentials* program, a fourteen-hour experiential program delivered in two days or over three half-days in live webinars. This program is designed to define and develop an understanding of the fundamental skills, processes, and benefits of coaching by leaders. The program is an excellent foundation for learning how a coaching mindset promotes growth and development for leaders and team members, resulting in much more than only improved performance. Graduates of *Leaders Who Coach: Essentials* can continue to build their capacity to coach by engaging in our leader-mentor coaching circles, Advanced Programs (*Strength-Based Coaching, Coaching to Improve Performance,* and *Coaching Teams etc.*) and their own executive coaching.

Learn more about our next *Leaders Who Coach: Essentials* program at www.leaderswhocoach.com or contact Jan Salisbury at info@leaderswhocoach.com.

CPSIA information can be obtained
at www.ICGtesting.com
Printed in the USA
BVHW051251251022
650240BV00004B/214